Edexcel International GCSE Economics

Revision Guide

Rob Jones

PEARSON

Published by Pearson Education Limited, Edinburgh Gate, Harlow, Essex, CM20 2JE.

www.pearsonglobalschools.com

Copies of official specifications for all Edexcel qualifications may be found on the Edexcel website: www.edexcel.com

Text © Pearson Education Limited 2013
Edited by Sheila Cameron
Proofread by Jim Caunter
Original design by Richard Ponsford
Typeset by Phoenix Photosetting
Original illustrations © Pearson Education Limited 2013
Indexed by Indexing Specialists (UK) Ltd.

The right of Robert Jones to be identified as author of this work has been asserted by him in accordance with the Copyright, Designs and Patents Act 1988.

First published 2013

20 19 18 17 16 15

10 9 8 7 6 5 4 3

British Library Cataloguing in Publication Data
A catalogue record for this book is available from the British Library

ISBN 978 1 446 90573 9

Acknowledgements
The author and publisher would like to thank the following individuals and organisations for permission to reproduce photographs:

(Key: b-bottom; c-centre; l-left; r-right; t-top)

Alamy Images: Jon Arnold Images Ltd 45bl; **Fotolia.com:** Gary 19cr, pedrosala e book (Wind Farm), Ssogras 69br; **Getty Images:** AFP 89br, e book (drought), e book (eggs), Andrew Watson 59br, Andy Sacks 27cr, e book (Car engine), Bloomberg via Getty Images 41br, e book (Warehouse), Bloomberg via Getty Images 41br, e book (Warehouse), Christopher Pillitz 33br, Getty Images 3br, Hans-Peter Merten 43br, Image Source e book (shoes), PhotoAlto / Isabelle Rozenbaum 81br, Ruy Barbosa Pinto e book (train), TAO Images Limited 9t

All other images © Pearson Education

In some instances we have been unable to trace the owners of copyright material, and we would appreciate any information that would enable us to do so. Every effort has been made to contact copyright holders of material reproduced in this book. Any omissions will be rectified in subsequent printings if notice is given to the publishers.

Websites
Pearson Education Limited is not responsible for the content of any external internet sites. It is essential for tutors to preview each website before using it in class so as to ensure that the URL is still accurate, relevant and appropriate. We suggest that tutors bookmark useful websites and consider enabling students to access them through the school/college intranet.

A note from the publisher
While the publishers have made every attempt to ensure that advice on the qualification and its assessment is accurate, the official specification and associated assessment guidance materials are the only authoritative source of information and should always be referred to for definitive guidance.

Edexcel examiners have not contributed to any sections in this resource relevant to examination papers for which they have responsibility.

Contents

How to use this revision guide

This revision guide is designed to help you with your revision. It contains:

- A summary of the important knowledge that you need for your exam. Knowledge is presented concisely in diagrams, tables and bullet points. Each chapter links up exactly with the Edexcel International GCSE Economics Student text book and the Edexcel International GCSE Economics specification.

- You will find a *Worked Example* in every chapter which shows how to write an answer to a range of questions from recent exam papers or exam-style questions.

- There are also some *Revision Questions* at the end of each chapter for you to practise. These are often exam-style questions. Examples of full written suggested answers to these questions can be found on the accompanying e-book, along with interactive quizzes and worksheets to help you revise.

- Every chapter contains a *Top tip* which may relate to the question in the Worked Example or to some important issue covered in the chapter.

- There is a *Key information* box in every chapter, which provides a range of different information, definitions and economic facts.

- The *Glossary* explains key words students should understand. All glossary terms have been made bold the first time they appear in the book.

- This revision guide is probably best used with the Edexcel International GCSE Economics Student text book at your side. This will obviously provide you with more detailed explanations if you require them.

Revision guidelines

Introduction

- The quality of your revision will affect how well you do in the exam. If you work hard during the revision period, and use effective revision activities, you may receive a better grade.

- Different people learn, and organise their revision, in different ways. If you follow the guidelines set out here, you are likely to be prepared better for your exam. However, you must decide which of these guidelines will support your personal approach to revision.

- The first thing to do is to plan your revision. Planning is *very* important. It will involve preparing a revision timetable. This will ensure that your revision is organised and that your time is not wasted.

Planning a revision timetable

Ask a teacher or parent to help you with this important task.

- You need to decide how much time you will spend revising. Many students begin their serious revision about six to eight weeks before the exam. However, this may not suit your circumstances. The earlier you begin revising though, the more time you will have for each subject.

- You need to divide the total revision time by the number of subjects that you are studying. You may decide to give each subject the same amount of time. Or, you might give certain subjects more time than others. This might be because these subjects are more important to you or because you need to spend more time on them.

- Your revision timetable could be prepared on a spreadsheet. Each day could be divided into *revision periods*—of say one hour. This does not mean that you will spend the whole hour working. You may need a 10 minute break in every hour.

- In each revision period you need to allocate a section of work from the specification. Each section should be of roughly the same length.

- Sections of work may be based on the chapters from the revision guide book. For example, each section might be one or two chapters in the book.

- Do not set yourself too much work in each revision period. This is because if you continually fail to complete what you have planned, you may become disheartened and stressed.

- It will be helpful to build in some breathing spaces. These will be empty revision periods which you can use if you do not keep up with your planned revision timetable. You might be wise to have a day, or half a day, off each week too. This will help you to refresh and the break is something to look forward to enjoying.

- It might take some time to draw up your realistic timetable. However, it will be well worth the effort. You will know what you are doing each day, and you can track your progress. Once you are happy with your timetable, you should try very hard follow it.

Revision activities

What you actually do in your revision periods is important. Although reading your notes and the text book will be helpful, reading on its own is not the best way to revise. It is boring and your concentration will suffer. You need to do some revision activities. There are some suggestions below. They will help you to:

- remember information
- develop the skills you need to obtain high grades
- concentrate more and waste less time
- build your confidence by reaching your targets.

1. Summarising

One way to remember information is to summarise it when you are going through your notes or text book. This revision guide does already contain a summary of the information that you need. However, you may wish to reduce the volume of information even further. You are more likely to remember information that you have written down. Summarising will generally involve making lists of key points from each chapter or section of work. Some tips on summarising might be to:

- use headings, sub-headings, definitions and key points for your summaries
- keep writing to a minimum
- summarise information on cards and use highlighter pens for key words, terms and formulae.

2. Producing visual memory aids

Another way to remember information is to produce some visual materials. Visual material will provide you with a 'picture' of information. Some people find it easier to remember visual information. Some examples are given below.

Spider diagrams, for example the 'Macroeconomic objectives' diagram on p. 60.

Family trees, for example the 'The role of entrepreneurs' diagram on p. 32.

Flow diagrams, for example the 'The process of price determination' diagram on p. 2.

Tables, for example the 'The use of fiscal policy to achieve macroeconomic objectives' table on p. 77.

Supply and demand diagrams, for example the 'Market equilibrium' diagram on p. 12.

3. Knowledge tests

An important part of the revision process is to find out how much you know. Some examples of testing methods are outlined below.

- **Multiple-choice questions**—there are quite a few in both the Student Book and the Revision Guide. There are also more in the Student Quizzes and Worksheets which can be found on the eText accompanying this revision guide.

- **Use summary cards**—rewrite from memory the information that you have written on summary cards. The more often you do this, the more your knowledge will build.

- **Definition tests**—use the glossary of terms to test your knowledge of the key terms in each chapter. Write out the definitions and check to see whether you have got them right.

4. Answer revision questions

- The *Revision Questions* at the end of each chapter are mainly exam-style questions. If you answer them, it will help you to strengthen your understanding of the material covered in the chapter. It will give you valuable practice at answering questions like the ones in your exam.

- You can also return to the Student Book and answer the questions at the end of each chapter. It does not matter if you have practised some of these questions before. Answering them again will give a boost to your learning. Hopefully, the quality of your answers will improve.

- There are fully written *suggested answers* to all of these questions.

5. Use past exam papers

- It is vital to look at past exam papers for Edexcel International GCSE Economics. You need to know what to expect when you sit your exam. More information about this exam paper is given in the Examination Preparation section at the end of this book.

- You need to answer all of the questions on the exam paper. The more past papers you look at, the better prepared you will be.

- Ideally, you should sit at least one mock Edexcel International GCSE Economics exam. This is the best way to find out how much you have learned. You can identify your weaknesses and then work on overcoming them.

6. Other activities

- Some people learn by reading information aloud. If you record what you have read aloud, you can play it back and listen to the information. This can add variety to revision and help your concentration. You could listen to recordings when you are doing something else, such as travelling or going for a walk.

- Make simple posters of key information, such as supply and demand diagrams. Place them in prominent places so that you keep seeing them.

- Work with friends or relatives. You and your friends can test each other, and members of your family can test you. However, you must be careful not to waste time!

Things to do and not to do for revision

To do

1. Start revising at least six to eight weeks before the exam.

2. You must prepare a timetable and stick to it.

3. Make your revision environment comfortable.

4. Set achievable targets each day. Reaching targets will help to motivate you.

5. Take regular breaks—10 to 15 minutes every hour.

6. You **must** ask for help when you are stuck. Ask a friend or a teacher.

7. Eat regular meals and take exercise during your revision.

8. Ensure that you have something to look forward to each day (for example meet a friend) and each week (for example a day or half a day off).

Not to do

1. Do not leave revision to the last minute—you **will** regret it if you do!

2. Do not avoid topics that you dislike or that you find hard.

3. Do not rely just on reading—use some of the suggested revision activities.

4. Do not continue revising when you are exhausted. There's no point. Rest. Start again in the morning.

5. Do not become distracted—learn how to say no! Follow your timetable.

6. Do not become too stressed—it's pointless. You can only do your best.

PART 1 Demand and supply

Chapter 1: **The market system**

What is a market?

- A **market** exists when buyers and sellers communicate and exchange goods for money.

- In some markets **trade** occurs in units such as shops, malls, market squares or kiosks where sellers display goods for buyers.

- Other markets exist when trading is done over the telephone, using newspapers, through mail order or online.

> Markets also exist for services. For example, traders may provide services such as driving instruction, gardening, transport or hairdressing. Customers pay service providers for the work carried out.

The functions of a market system

Markets operate together like a system. This **market system**, sometimes called the **price mechanism**, performs two functions.

Price determination

One of the most important things buyers and sellers discuss when trading is the price of the goods or services.

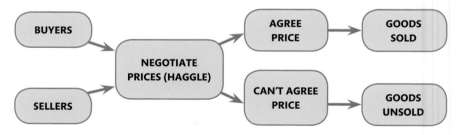

Figure 1.1 *The process of price determination.*

> In some markets there is no negotiation. For example, in many shops buyers are expected to pay the price displayed on the label. However, if they don't, the unsold goods send a signal to a seller. Either they reduce the price or they are left with the unsold goods. This shows that communication between buyers and sellers still takes place.

Resource allocation

The market system helps to allocate a nation's resources. Resources flow from declining markets where prices are falling into thriving markets where prices are rising.

Figure 1.2 *The process of resource allocation.*

Supply and Demand

In markets there are buyers and sellers.

- **Demand** (represented by buyers) is the amount of a good that will be bought at given prices over a period of time.

- **Supply** is the amount of a good that sellers are prepared to sell at given prices over a period of time.

Prices are determined by the interaction of supply and demand. Their effects on prices are summarised as follows:

RISING DEMAND ⟶ HIGHER PRICES

FALLING DEMAND ⟶ LOWER PRICES

RISING SUPPLY ⟶ LOWER PRICES

FALLING SUPPLY ⟶ HIGHER PRICES

> Markets can fail. For example, a lack of competition in a market often means that buyers pay higher prices and have less choice.

Worked Example

Explain what is meant by a market. (3)

> A market is a set of arrangements that allows buyers and sellers to communicate and exchange goods and services. For example, there is a market for second-hand cars. They may be sold by dealers from showrooms, or through sales pitches. Buyers can view cars and negotiate prices with the seller. Today, cars can also be traded online.

TOP TIP

It is useful to include an example when answering a question.

Revision Questions

Some goods, such as property, antiques and works of art, are sold at auctions. This is where buyers bid against each other to buy goods. The person who makes the highest bid wins the right to buy the goods.

1 Define (*a*) demand (*b*) price. (2)

2 How are prices determined in the market described above? (3)

3 Explain how the market system allocates a nation's resources. (4)

Chapter 2: **The demand curve**

A demand schedule

The amount of a product demanded at different prices can be presented in a table. This is called a demand schedule. Figure 2.1 shows a demand schedule for a product.

Price (US$)	2.5	3	4	5	7	10
Quantity demanded (units)	1300	1000	700	500	300	200

Figure 2.1 *Demand schedule for a product.*

The demand curve

- A **demand curve** is formed if the prices and quantities shown in Figure 2.1 are plotted on a graph and joined with a line. This is shown in Figure 2.2.

- A demand curve shows the quantity demanded at any given price. For example if the price is US$7 the quantity demanded is 300 units.

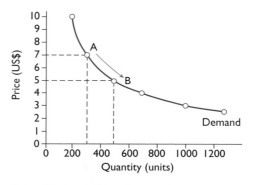

Figure 2.2 *Demand curve for a product.*

> When drawing a demand curve, remember that price is shown on the vertical axis and the quantity demanded is shown on the horizontal axis.

The slope of the demand curve

The demand curve nearly always slopes down from left to right. This means that price and quantity demanded are **inversely** related. So that:

- when prices go up demand will fall

- when prices go down demand will rise.

Movement along the demand curve

- When price changes there is a **movement along** the demand curve.

- In Figure 2.2, when the price falls from US$7 to US$5 we move along the demand curve from A to B. Demand rises from 300 to 500 units.

Straight line demand curves

It is common to show a demand curve as a straight line. This simplifies the drawing of demand curves. It makes it easier to understand diagrams. An example is shown in Figure 2.3.

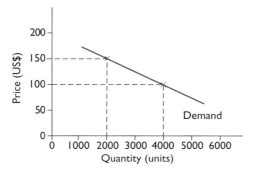

Figure 2.3 *A straight line demand curve showing the demand for an item of furniture.*

Worked Example

Explain the relationship between price and the quantity demanded. **(4)**

There is an inverse relationship between the price of a product and the quantity demanded. This means that price and quantity move in opposite directions. For example, when prices go up demand will fall, and when prices go down demand will rise. This relationship means that the demand curve slopes down from left to right.

TOP TIP

Remember that demand curves are shown as straight lines because it is easier to draw them that way and to understand the diagrams.

Revision Questions

The demand schedule for a product is shown in Figure 2.4.

Price (€)	10	15	20	25	30	35	40
Quantity demanded (units)	700	600	500	400	300	200	100

Figure 2.4 *Demand schedule for a product.*

1 Draw a demand curve using the information in Figure 2.4. **(4)**

Use your graph to answer question 2.

2 **(a)** The seller currently charges €22.50 for this product. How much would be demanded at this price? **(1)**

(b) What happens to the quantity demanded when the price is increased from €22.50 to €30? **(1)**

3 Why does the demand curve slope down from left to right? **(2)**

Chapter 3: **Factors that affect demand**

Factors affecting demand

Income

- When income rises, demand for most goods will rise.
- Income is more likely to affect the demand for non-essential products such as holidays, cars and furniture.

> Most goods are **normal goods**. This means that demand increases when incomes rise. A few goods are **inferior goods** where demand falls when incomes rise. For example used or second-hand goods.

Advertising

- Businesses use advertising campaigns and promotions to increase demand for their products.
- Large amounts of money are used to advertise both goods and services.

Population (growth and structure)

- As the population grows, demand will rise. Population can grow if the birth rate increases, or the death rate falls, or if immigration rises.
- Demand will also be affected by the structure of the population. Figure 3.1 gives some examples.

Distribution	Definition	Effect on demand—An example
Age	The population is made up of different age groups.	Children buy toys, but the over sixties buy more cruises.
Gender	The population is divided into males and females.	Females buy more cosmetics, but males buy more neckties.
Geographical	The population is divided into different regions.	Demand is higher for schools in urban areas than in rural areas.
Ethnic	Different ethnic groups are part of the population.	Ethnic groups demand specific products linked to their culture.

Figure 3.1 *Demand and population structure.*

Tastes and fashion

- Demand is affected by changes in consumer tastes and fashion.
- For example there has been a growth in demand for health foods in some countries.

Prices of substitutes

- Many goods have **substitutes**. For example, substitutes for a can of Coca-Cola might include brands such as Pepsi.
- The price of substitutes will affect demand. If the price of Pepsi is reduced, demand for Coca-Cola might fall.

Prices of complements

- **Complementary goods** are purchased together, such as cars and car insurance.
- If the price of cars rises, the demand for car insurance may fall.

A shift in the demand curve

- For a change in price there is a movement along the demand curve.
- A change in any other factor will be shown by a **shift of the demand curve**.
- D_1 in Figure 3.2 is for cars. A rise in income will increase the demand for cars and will shift the demand curve to the right to D_2.
- A fall in income may reduce demand. This is shown by a shift of the demand curve to the left to D_3.

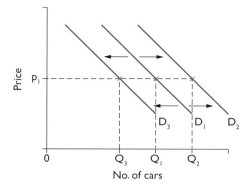

Figure 3.2 *A shift in the demand curve for cars.*

Worked Example

In 2009, Russian tea experts forecast that when incomes in Russia fall due to recession, people will drink more tea. This suggests that in Russia tea is

- **A**   a normal good
- **B**   a luxury good
- **C**   an inferior good
- **D**   a complementary good.   *(1)*

© Edexcel Question paper, June 2011

C is the answer. Demand for an inferior good will rise if incomes fall. In Russia the demand for tea is expected to rise as incomes fall due to the recession.

TOP TIP

It will be easier to answer this question if you have learnt how to define all of the terms listed here as possible answers.

Revision Questions

Figure 3.3 shows the world demand curve for rice

1 Draw two diagrams to show the effect on the demand curve:
- *(a)* of an increase in the global population; *(3)*
- *(b)* if people eat more meat instead of rice. *(3)*

2 Assess the effects of an ageing population on the firms in an economy. *(6)*

Question 2 © Edexcel Question paper, June 2011

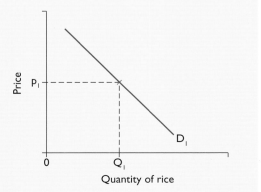

Figure 3.3 *World demand for rice.*

Chapter 4: **The supply curve**

A supply schedule

The amount of a product supplied at different prices can be presented in a table. This is a **supply schedule**. Figure 4.1 shows a supply schedule for a product.

Price (US$)	2	3	4	6	9
Quantity supplied (units)	200	600	900	1100	1200

Figure 4.1 *Supply schedule for a product.*

The supply curve

- If the prices and quantities shown in Figure 4.1 are plotted on a graph and joined with a line a **supply curve** is formed. This is shown in Figure 4.2.

- A supply curve shows the quantity supplied at any given price. For example when the price is US$4 the quantity supplied is 900 units.

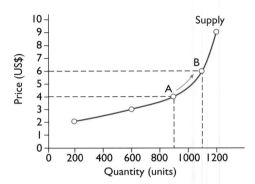

Figure 4.2 *Supply curve for a product.*

The slope of the supply curve

The supply curve normally slopes up from left to right. This means that:

- when prices rise supply will rise

- when prices fall supply will fall.

> The reason for the relationship between supply and price is that if prices are rising, businesses are willing to supply more of a good. This is because they may make more profit.

Movement along the supply curve

- When price changes there is a **movement along** the supply curve.

- In Figure 4.2, when the price rises from US$4 to US$6, we move along the supply curve from A to B. Supply increases from 900 to 1100 units.

> As with demand curves, supply curves are usually shown as straight lines. This makes it easier to draw diagrams and to understand them.

Fixed supply

- Supply may be fixed, which means that sellers cannot increase supply even when prices rise. As a result, the supply curve will be vertical.

- The supply of seats at the Beijing Olympic Stadium is fixed at 80,000. Even if prices rise from P_1 to P_2 supply cannot be increased above 80,000 seats.

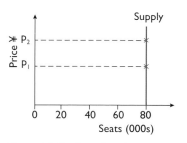

Figure 4.3 *Fixed supply – the Beijing Olympic Stadium.*

Worked Example

Figure 4.4 shows the supply curve for a product.

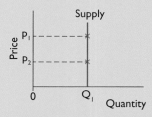

Figure 4.4 *The supply curve for a product.*

(a) What happens to the quantity supplied when price falls from P_1 to P_2? *(1)*

(b) Explain a possible reason for your answer in (a). *(2)*

1 **(a)** When price falls from P_1 to P_2 there is no change in supply. Supply stays at Q_1.

(b) Supply cannot change when price changes because supply is fixed. This means that sellers cannot reduce supply when prices fall.

TOP TIP

Most supply curves slope up from left to right. But remember, when supply is fixed the supply curve will be vertical.

Revision Questions

1 Which of the following statements is **true** about the supply curve?

   A All supply curves are vertical.

   B A supply curve shows the relationship between supply and demand.

   C A supply curve shows the amount supplied by producers at given prices.

   D A supply curve will shift to the right if price falls. *(1)*

Price (US$)	10	20	30	40
Quantity supplied (000s)	100	300	500	700

Figure 4.5 *The supply schedule for a product.*

2 Draw a supply curve using the information in Figure 4.5. *(4)*

3 **(a)** How much would be supplied in the market if the price was US$25? *(1)*

   (b) What happens to the quantity supplied when price rises from US$25 to US$30? *(1)*

Chapter 5: **Factors that affect supply**

Factors affecting supply

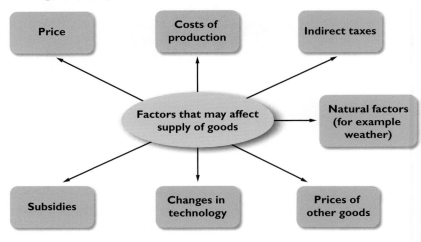

Figure 5.1 *The factors that may affect the supply of goods.*

Costs of production

- If production costs such as wages and raw materials rise, sellers may reduce supply because their profits will be reduced.
- If costs fall, supply increases because production becomes more profitable.

> The availability of resources, such as workers or materials, will also affect supply. If there is a shortage, producers may struggle to supply the market.

Indirect taxes

- **Indirect taxes** are taxes on spending such as Value Added Tax and excise duties.
- When indirect taxes are imposed or increased, supply will fall because indirect taxes represent a cost to firms.
- If indirect taxes are reduced, supply will increase because costs are lower.

Subsidies

- A **subsidy** is a government grant given to producers to encourage production of a certain good.
- If a producer receives a subsidy, supply will increase because costs are reduced.
- Subsidies are used in countries such as Norway, Korea and Taiwan to support their fishing industries.

Changes in technology

- Over time, businesses can use new technology such as machinery and new production techniques.
- New technology increases supply because costs fall. For example new solar cell technology is being used to cut energy costs.

Natural factors

- Natural factors such as the weather can affect the supply of some goods—particularly agricultural products.
- Good growing conditions improve crop yields which increase supply. Poor weather may cause shortages and supply may be reduced, which forces prices up.

The prices of other goods

- Some producers can switch production from one product to another. For example farmers can often produce a number of different crops.
- Firms may switch production to a workable alternative if its price starts to rise. As a result, the supply of this alternative product will increase, while the supply of the existing product will fall.

A shift in the supply curve

- When price changes there is a **movement along the supply curve**.
- A change in a factor other than price is shown by a **shift in the supply curve**.
- S_1 in Figure 5.2 is the supply curve for biofuel. A new subsidy increases the supply of biofuel and shifts the supply curve to the right to S_2.

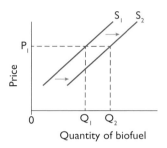

Figure 5.2 *A shift in the supply curve for biofuel.*

Worked Example

Figure 5.3 shows a shift in the supply of cars.

1 State **two** factors which may have shifted supply from S_1 to S_2. *(2)*

| 1 | New technology |
| 2 | Lower energy costs |

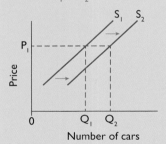

Figure 5.3 *A shift in the supply of cars.*

TOP TIP

In questions like this there are often several possible answers. Here, other answers might be lower wages, lower rent, a subsidy or lower indirect taxes.

Revision Questions

In 2012, a warm month of March in the United States was followed by a short cold spell in April. This caused a failure in the apple crop. The apple harvest was about 10 per cent of the normal yield.

1 Draw a diagram to show the effect on the supply of apples of the adverse growing conditions. *(4)*

2 Explain the likely effect of the poor harvest on the price of apples in the United States. *(4)*

3 Explain the effect of a subsidy to apple growers on the supply of apples in the United States? *(4)*

Chapter 6: **Market equilibrium**

Equilibrium price

- On a graph, the **equilibrium price** is where supply and demand are equal.

- In Figure 6.1, the equilibrium price in the market is £25.

- The quantity demanded and the quantity supplied are equal at 300 units.

Total revenue

- Total revenue is the amount of money generated from the sale of output.

- Total revenue = Price × Quantity **or** TR = P × Q.

- In Figure 6.1 the total revenue is shown by the shaded area. It is:

$$TR = P \times Q = £25 \times 300 = £7,500$$

Shifts in supply and demand curves

The equilibrium price will change if there are changes in supply or demand.

- If demand increases, the demand curve shifts to the right. Both price and quantity will rise. Figure 6.2 shows this. The opposite will happen if demand falls.

- If supply increases, the supply curve shifts to the right. Price will fall and quantity will rise. Figure 6.3 shows this. The opposite will happen if supply falls.

> It is possible for both supply and demand to change. The effect on equilibrium price depends on the size and direction of the changes in supply and demand.

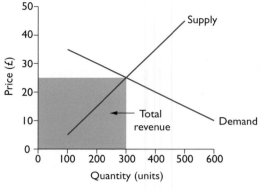

Figure 6.1 *Market equilibrium.*

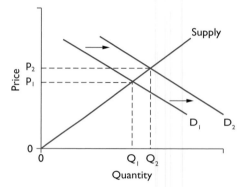

Figure 6.2 *Shift in demand.*

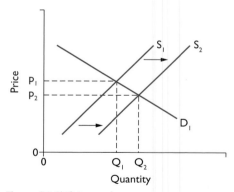

Figure 6.3 *Shift in supply.*

Excess demand and excess supply

- If the price is set below equilibrium, demand will be greater than supply and there will be **excess demand**. There will be a shortage of goods.

- If the price is set above equilibrium, supply will be greater than demand and there will be **excess supply**. Goods will remain unsold.

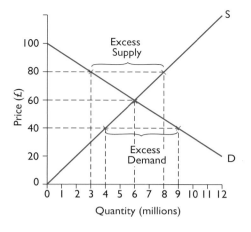

Figure 6.4 *Excess demand and excess supply.*

Worked Example

Figure 6.5 shows the world demand and supply of tea in 2008.

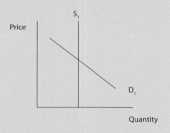

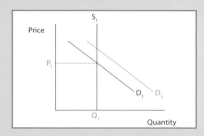

Figure 6.5

(a) On Figure 6.5 label the equilibrium price, P_1, and equilibrium quantity, Q_1. *(1)*

(b) In 2009, the demand for tea in China and Russia rose. On Figure 6.5 draw a new demand curve, D_2, to illustrate this growth in demand. *(1)*

Adapted from Edexcel Question paper, June 2011

TOP TIP ✓

Use a pencil when drawing diagrams so that you can erase any mistakes with a eraser.

Revision Questions

The market for a product is shown by the supply and demand curves in Figure 6.6.

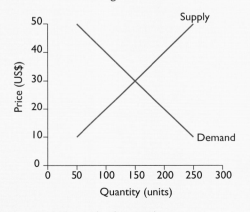

Figure 6.6 *The market for a product.*

1 What is the equilibrium price?
   a) US$10
   b) US$20
   c) US$30
   d) None of the above *(1)*

2 Calculate the total revenue at the equilibrium price. *(2)*

3 If the price was US$40 there would be excess supply in the market. Explain what this means. *(4)*

Chapter 7: **Price elasticity of demand**

What is price elasticity of demand (PED)?

- **Price elasticity of demand** measures the responsiveness of demand to a change in price.

- For some goods, a price change will cause a more than proportionate change in demand.

- For other goods, a price change will cause a less than proportionate change in demand.

Inelastic and elastic demand

The demand curves for products X and Y in Figure 7.1 have different slopes. At a price of £4, demand for both products is 25,000 units. However, when the price falls to £3, the changes in demand are different for each product. Figure 7.2 summarises the effects.

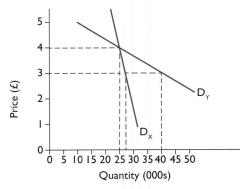

Figure 7.1 *Demand curves for two products X and Y.*

Product	Demand curve	Demand	Price change	Change in demand
X	Steep	**INELASTIC**	£4 to £3 (−25%)	**Small** 25,000 to 27,000 (8%)
Y	Flat	**ELASTIC**	£4 to £3 (−25%)	**Large** 25,000 to 40,000 (60%)

Figure 7.2 *Inelastic and elastic demand.*

Calculating the value of price elasticity of demand

$$\text{Price elasticity of demand} = \frac{\text{Percentage change in quantity demanded}}{\text{Percentage change in price}}$$

For product X in Figure 7.1,

PED is: = 8% ÷ −25% = −0.32

For product Y in Figure 7.1,

PED is: = 60% ÷ −25% = −2.4

> Both answers are minus. This is because the price fell by 25 per cent (from £4 to £3). Since the price change was negative, a minus sign must be shown. **Please note that you will NOT have to calculate price elasticity in the exam. The examples here are for illustration only.**

Interpreting the value of elasticity

- If the value of PED is negative and less than 1, demand is said to be **inelastic**. Demand for product X is **price inelastic** (−0.32).

- If the value of PED is negative and greater than 1, demand is said to be **elastic**. Demand for product Y is **price elastic** (−2.4).

Price elasticity and the slope of the demand curve

- For product X in Figure 7.1, the demand curve is steep. This is common for goods which have inelastic demand.

- For product Y, the demand curve is less steep. Goods which have elastic demand tend to have less steep demand curves.

A perfectly inelastic demand curve, where PED is zero, is vertical. A perfectly elastic demand curve, where PED is infinite, is horizontal.

Factors affecting price elasticity of demand

Factor	Description	PED	Examples
Number of substitutes	Few substitutes	**INELASTIC**	Petrol or tobacco
	Many substitutes	**ELASTIC**	Chocolate bars
Degree of necessity	Essential goods	**INELASTIC**	Food or fuel
	Non-essential goods	**ELASTIC**	Holidays or computer games
Proportion of income	Small proportion	**INELASTIC**	Stamps or pencils
	Large proportion	**ELASTIC**	Consumer durables

Figure 7.3 *Factors affecting PED.*

Worked Example

The demand for flour is price inelastic, whereas the demand for chocolate is price elastic.
Do you agree with this statement? Give reasons for your answer. **(6)**

© *Edexcel Question paper, May 2012*

Demand for flour is likely to be inelastic because it is used to make bread, which is an essential good in many countries. A price change for flour would have little impact on the demand for flour. The change in demand would be proportionately less than the change in price. In contrast, the demand for chocolate is likely to be elastic. A price change will cause a more than proportionate change in demand for chocolate. This is because it is a non-essential product. People can live without it if the price rises. However, there may be substitutes for flour such as rice. This might make flour more elastic. However, it is not likely to be as elastic as chocolate, which probably has far more substitutes.

TOP TIP

To receive 4 marks you must refer to both flour and chocolate. To receive 6 marks you must evaluate the statement in the question, by discussing the possibility that flour has substitutes, for example.

Revision Questions

1   Define price elasticity of demand. **(2)**

2   In Figure 7.4, when the price falls from US$100 to US$90, what is the price elasticity of demand?

    A   PED is zero

    B   PED is infinite

    C   Demand is price elastic

    D   Demand is price inelastic **(1)**

3   Explain **two** reasons why demand for a product might be elastic. **(4)**

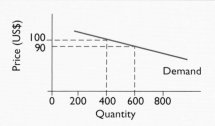

Figure 7.4 *Demand for a product.*

Chapter 8: **Price elasticity of supply**

What is price elasticity of supply (PES)?

- **Price elasticity of supply** measures the responsiveness of supply to a change in price.

- For some goods, a price change causes a more than proportionate change in supply. For other goods, a price change causes a less than proportionate change in supply.

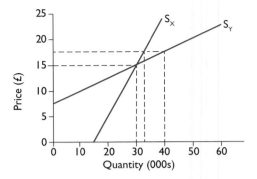

Figure 8.1 *Supply curves for two products X and Y.*

Inelastic and elastic supply

The supply curves for products X and Y in Figure 8.1 have different slopes. At a price of £15, supply for both products is 30,000 units. However, when the price rises to £18 the changes in supply are different for each product. Figure 8.2 summarises the effects.

Product	Supply curve	Supply	Price change	Change in supply
X	Steep	**INELASTIC**	£15 to £18 (20%)	**Small** 30,000 to 33,000 (10%)
Y	Flat	**ELASTIC**	£15 to £18 (20%)	**Large** 30,000 to 42,000 (40%)

Figure 8.2 *Inelastic and elastic supply.*

Calculating the value of price elasticity of supply

$$\text{Price elasticity of supply} = \frac{\text{Percentage change in quantity supplied}}{\text{Percentage change in price}}$$

For product X in Figure 8.1,

PES is: = 10% ÷ 20% = 0.5

For product Y in Figure 8.1,

PES is: = 40% ÷ 20% = 2

> These calculations are for illustration purposes. **You do NOT need to calculate price elasticity of supply in the exam**.

Interpreting the value of price elasticity of supply

- If the value of PES is positive and less than 1, supply is said to be **inelastic**. Supply for product X is **price inelastic** (0.5).

- If the value of PES is positive and greater than 1, supply is said to be **elastic**. Supply for product Y is **price elastic** (2).

Price elasticity and the slope of the supply curve

- For product X in Figure 8.1, the supply curve is steep. This is common for goods which have inelastic supply.

- For product Y, the supply curve is much flatter. Goods which have elastic supply tend to have flatter supply curves.

A perfectly inelastic supply curve, where PES is zero, is vertical. A perfectly elastic supply curve, where PES is infinite, is horizontal.

Factors affecting price elasticity of supply

Time is important for the price elasticity of supply. Supply is price elastic if producers can increase supply quickly and it is inelastic if they cannot.

Factor	Description	PES	Examples
Stock levels	Low or zero stock levels	**INELASTIC**	Perishable goods
	High or flexible stocks	**ELASTIC**	Manufactured goods
Production speed	Slow production	**INELASTIC**	Agricultural goods
	Speedy production	**ELASTIC**	Manufactured goods
Spare capacity	High or full capacity	**INELASTIC**	Fixed-capacity producers
	Spare capacity	**ELASTIC**	Flexible-capacity producers

Figure 8.3 *Factors affecting PES.*

Worked Example

It is always more difficult to increase the supply of agricultural goods than manufactured goods. Do you agree with this statement? Explain your answer. **(6)**

© *Edexcel Question paper, June 2011*

The supply of agricultural goods is usually inelastic, which means that producers cannot increase supply quickly. One reason for this is that growing periods can be lengthy. For example it takes nearly a year to grow a crop of wheat. Also, it may be difficult to store agricultural goods, because they are perishable. The supply of manufactured goods is more elastic. This is because manufacturers can increase supply by speeding up production or releasing goods from stocks. However, if a manufacturer does not have any stocks, and is operating at full capacity, it may not be able increase supply. Therefore, the supply of manufactured goods could also be inelastic under certain circumstances.

TOP TIP ✓

To receive 4 marks you must discuss the supply of both agricultural goods and manufactured goods. For 6 marks you need to evaluate the statement by suggesting, for example, that there may be exceptions.

Revision Questions

1 In Figure 8.4 the price elasticity of supply of wheat is

    A perfectly elastic

    B perfectly inelastic

    C 2.5

    D infinite   *(1)*

2 The value of price elasticity of supply for wheat is zero. Explain what this means. *(4)*

3 A product has elastic supply. Explain **one** reason why this might be the case. *(4)*

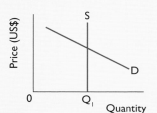

Figure 8.4 *Russian wheat market.*

Chapter 9: **Income elasticity**

What is income elasticity of demand?

Income elasticity of demand measures the responsiveness of demand to a change in income. Figure 9.1 shows income elasticity of demand for two products, X and Y.

Product	Change in income	Change in demand	Elasticity
X	5%	20% (More than proportionate)	Income elastic
Y	5%	4% (Less than proportionate)	Income inelastic

Figure 9.1 *Income elasticity for two products X and Y.*

Measuring income elasticity of demand

$$\text{Income elasticity of demand} = \frac{\text{Percentage change in quantity demanded}}{\text{Percentage change in income}}$$

For a product X, the income elasticity of demand is:

$= 20\% \div 5\% = 4$

For product Y, the income elasticity of demand is:

$= 4\% \div 5\% = 0.8$

> **You do NOT need to calculate income elasticity in the exam**. The calculations here are for illustration.

Interpreting the value of income elasticity of demand

- If the value of the income elasticity of demand is greater than 1 or less than −1, demand is **income elastic**. Demand for product X (4) is income elastic.

- If the value of income elasticity of demand is between 1 and −1, demand is **income inelastic**. Demand for product Y (0.8) is income inelastic.

Normal goods, inferior goods and income elasticity

- For a **normal good** income elasticity of demand will be **positive**. This means that when income rises demand will also rise, or if income falls demand will also fall.

- For an **inferior good** income elasticity of demand is **negative**. This means that when income rises demand will fall, and if income falls demand will rise.

- Products X and Y (above) are both normal goods because income elasticity of demand is positive.

Factors affecting income elasticity of demand

- If goods are **necessities** (basic goods such as food, fuel and water) demand is income inelastic.

- If goods are **luxuries** such as air travel, satellite television and fashion accessories demand is income elastic.

> It is argued that the demand for imported goods is income elastic because as developing nations become wealthier, their demand for imports rises significantly.

With reference to the income elasticity of demand, explain the difference between a normal good and an inferior good. **(4)**

© *Edexcel Question paper, June 2011*

For a normal good, income elasticity of demand is positive. This means that when income rises demand will also rise, or if income falls demand will also fall. For an inferior good, income elasticity of demand is negative. This means that when income rises demand will fall, or if income falls demand will rise. Supermarket 'own brands' may be regarded by some consumers as inferior goods.

TOP TIP

Be careful not to confuse income elasticity of demand with price elasticity of demand.

Figure 9.2 shows the income elasticity of demand (IED) for three products.

Product	IED
A	−0.4
B	0.8
C	2.4

Figure 9.2 *Income elasticity of demand for products A, B and C.*

1 Define income elasticity of demand. **(2)**

2 Which of the following statements is true? Product C is

    A price elastic

    B an inferior good

    C income inelastic

    D income elastic **(1)**

3 Demand for the product shown in the photograph is income elastic. Do you agree with this statement? Give reasons for your answer. **(4)**

Chapter 10: **Applications of elasticity**

Price elasticity and firms

- Firms want to know the effect of price changes on total revenue.

- Consider the demand curves for product A (inelastic) and product B (elastic) in Figure 10.1.

- When price is US$40, demand for both products is 20,000 units and total revenue is US$800,000 (US$40 × 20,000). What happens when price falls to US$30?

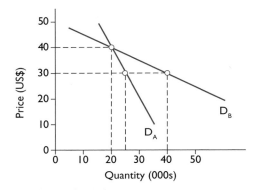

Figure 10.1 *The demand curves for two different products A and B.*

For product A

- **When P = US$30** TR = US$30 × 25,000 = US$750,000

- The price cut from US$40 to US$30 increases demand from 20,000 to 25,000 units. However, total revenue falls by US$50,000.

> WHEN DEMAND IS **INELASTIC** A PRICE CUT WILL **REDUCE** TOTAL REVENUE

For product B

- **When P = US$30** TR = US$30 × 40,000 = US$1,200,000

- The price cut from US$40 to US$30 increases demand from 20,000 to 40,000 units and total revenue rises by US$400,000.

> WHEN DEMAND IS **ELASTIC** A PRICE CUT WILL **INCREASE** TOTAL REVENUE

The effect of price changes on total revenue for different price elasticities is summarised in Figure 10.2.

Price elasticity	Value of elasticity	Price change	Effect on total revenue
Inelastic	Negative and <1	Decrease	Fall
Inelastic	Negative and <1	Increase	Rise
Elastic	Negative and >1	Decrease	Rise
Elastic	Negative and >1	Increase	Fall

Figure 10.2 *The effect of price changes on total revenue when demand is elastic and inelastic.*

Income elasticity and firms

- Firms will be interested in the effect of changes in income on demand.

- Firms with flexible resources and can switch from the production of one good to produce another. For example a manufacturer of plastic products may be able to switch production from household goods to toys.

- A rise in incomes may encourage the firm to make more toys if demand for toys is income elastic.

Price elasticity and the government

- Governments impose indirect taxes on goods which are price inelastic. This is because consumers cannot easily avoid buying them.

- Therefore, governments target necessities or goods with few substitutes.

> Popular targets for indirect taxes are petrol and tobacco because their demand is very price inelastic.

Worked Example

With reference to total revenue, explain what is meant by a *price inelastic demand curve*. **(4)**

© *Edexcel Question paper, May 2012*

ANSWER

If a product has an inelastic demand curve, then a price change will result in a less than proportionate change in the quantity demanded. This means that a price increase will lead to a less than proportionate fall in the quantity demanded. As a result, a price increase will raise total revenue. In contrast, a price cut will reduce total revenue. This is because when demand is price inelastic, total revenue will move in the same direction as the price change.

TOP TIP

In this answer 2 marks are awarded for giving a correct definition of price inelastic demand. Another 2 marks are given for explaining the relationship between elasticity, changes in price and the effect on total revenue.

Revision Questions

ZingCo produces a range of textile products in Binhai Industry Park, China. Demand for one of its garments is shown in Figure 10.3.

1 (a) Calculate the change in total revenue when the price is reduced from US$4 to US$3.50. **(4)**

   (b) Explain whether demand for the garment is price elastic or price inelastic. **(2)**

2 To what extent might income elasticity of demand be helpful to a firm like ZingCo? Give reasons for your answer. **(6)**

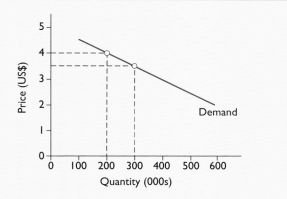

Figure 10.3 *Demand for a garment produced by ZingCo.*

PART 2 The role of the market in solving the economic problem

Chapter 11: Resolving scarcity

Finite resources and infinite wants

- Countries have a **finite** (limited) amount of resources such as water, minerals, plants and animals. Resources are said to be **scarce**.

- People have **needs** such as water, food, warmth, shelter and clothing.

- People also have **wants** such as more holidays and a bigger car.

- Wants are **infinite** (unlimited). Most people always want more.

The economic problem

The **basic economic problem** involves deciding how to allocate a nation's scarce resources between different uses. It is summarised in Figure 11.1.

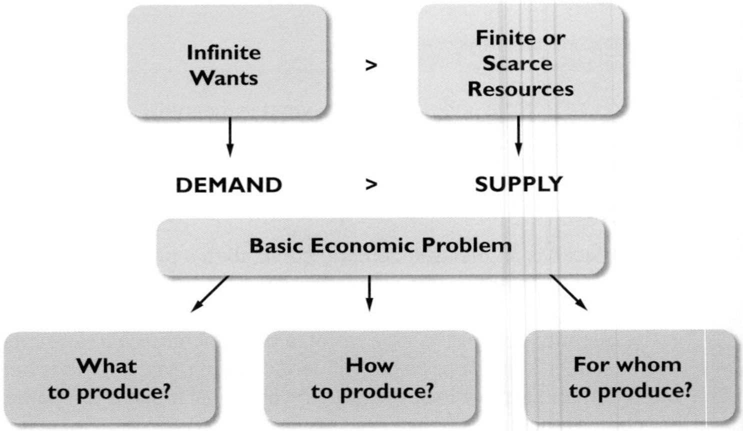

Solving the basic economic problem involves making some important decisions.

- **What to produce?** For example clothes, schools, military goods, cars or computers.

- **How to produce?** Which production methods should be used?

- **For whom to produce?** How should goods be shared?

Figure 11.1 *The basic economic problem.*

Choice and opportunity cost

- Individuals, firms and the government have to make a **choice** about how to use their resources.

- For example a firm with limited funds of US$10m may have to choose between (in order of preference) **1** Factory extension, **2** New product development or **3** Retraining workers.

- A sacrifice has to be made when making this choice. It is called the **opportunity cost**.

- If the factory extension is chosen, the opportunity cost will be the **benefit lost from the next best alternative**—that is, the benefit lost from not developing a new product.

> Individuals and governments will also incur opportunity costs. For example a government may have to choose between different items of expenditure such as education or road maintenance when allocating funds.

Production possibility curves

- A **production possibility curve (PPC)** shows how a country's resources can be used to produce different combinations of two goods.

- Figure 11.2 shows a PPC for a country which produces **consumer goods** (for example food and clothes) or **capital goods** (for example machinery and tools).

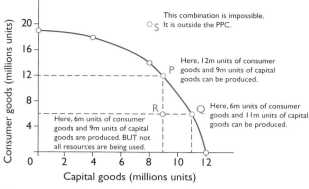

Figure 11.2 *A production possibility curve for a country.*

Opportunity cost and the PPC

- An opportunity cost is incurred when moving from one point to another on the PPC.

- In Figure 11.2, by moving from P to Q the production of capital goods rises from 9m to 11m units. But production of consumer goods falls from 12m to 6m units. To gain another 2m units of capital goods, 6m units of consumer goods are sacrificed. This lost production of consumer goods is the opportunity cost.

Worked Example

The opportunity cost of increasing production of capital goods from OA to OB is:

- **A** OC
- **B** CD
- **C** AB
- **D** OD   *(1)*

© Edexcel Sample Assessment Material

> **B** is the correct answer. When producing AB extra capital goods the production of CD consumer goods is sacrificed. This is the opportunity cost.

Figure 11.3 *A production possibility curve for a country.*

TOP TIP ✓
Opportunity cost is very important in economics. Make sure you can define the concept and apply it on PPCs.

Revision Questions

1 What is shown by a production possibility curve? *(2)*

2 Explain what is meant by the basic economic problem. *(4)*

3 Explain the effects of opportunity cost on a business. *(4)*

Chapter 12: **The mixed economy**

The public and private sectors in the economy

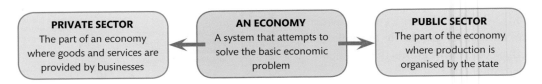

Figure 12.1 *Private and public sectors in an economy.*

Types of economy

- **Market economy** Private sector firms provide most of the goods and services, which are distributed by market forces.
- **Planned economy** Public sector organisations provide most of the goods and services, which are often sold in state-owned shops.
- **Mixed economy** Both private sector and public sector organisations provide goods and services.

The mixed economy

Most countries have mixed economies where production is shared between the private and the public sectors.

	Private sector	Public sector
What to produce?	Provides most goods such as food and clothes. The market system ensures that firms only produce goods that people want.	Provides goods such as education and healthcare, because firms in the private sector may under-provide them.
How to produce?	Goods are provided by profit-making businesses. Competing firms choose production methods that maximise quality and minimise costs.	Services are provided by government organisations. They decide how services should be provided efficiently.
For whom to produce?	Goods are allocated by the market system and sold to anyone who can afford them.	Services are provided free to everyone and are paid for mainly from taxes.

Figure 12.2 *Production in a mixed economy.*

Efficiency

Since resources are scarce, economies should ensure that production is **efficient**.

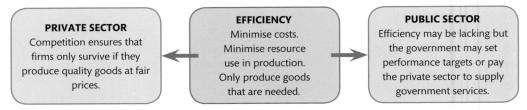

Figure 12.3 *Efficiency in the private and public sectors.*

Market failure

Sometimes **market failure** occurs and resources are not allocated efficiently. Examples include:

- **Negative externalities** These are costs, such as pollution, imposed by businesses on society.

- **Lack of competition** In markets dominated by one firm, consumers may be exploited. This leads to higher prices and less choice.

- **Missing markets** Public goods, such as defence or policing, are not provided by the private sector.

- **Merit goods** Such as education and healthcare are underprovided by the private sector.

> The public sector must deal with market failure. For example it must provide public and merit goods, ensure that competition exists and penalise those who impose costs on society.

Worked Example

Botswana has a mixed economy. Identify **two** characteristics of a mixed economy. **(2)**

> 1 Goods are produced by both the private and the public sector.
>
> 2 Market failure can exist in a mixed economy.

TOP TIP

In questions like this there is no need to give explanations. You will be wasting your time if you do.

Revision Questions

Most countries have mixed economies. However, the size of the private sector in relation to the public sector can vary.

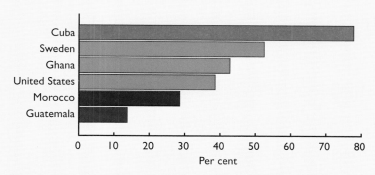

Figure 12.4 *Government expenditure as a percentage of national income for several countries 2011.*

1 What evidence is there in Figure 12.4 to suggest that the government provides most goods and services in Cuba? **(2)**

2 Explain how most goods and services are allocated in Guatemala. **(4)**

3 The private sector should produce all of the goods and services in the economy. Do you agree with this statement? Give reasons for your answer. **(6)**

PART 3 The labour market: an example of a market in a mixed economy

Chapter 13: The division of labour

Labour

- Labour is a term used to describe people available for work.
- People available for work in a country represent the **working population**.

> Globally, the supply of labour is increasing. This is because the population of the world is growing so fast. It is expected to grow from 6.76 billion in 2008 to 9 billion by 2040.

The division of labour

- Production processes are often broken down into small parts and each worker is given a specific task. This is called the **division of labour**.
- It allows people to concentrate on the task or skill at which they are best. For example on a car assembly line tasks might include engine installation, seat installation, wheel installation and many other assembly tasks.

The advantages of the division of labour to the firm and the worker

	Advantages to the firm	Advantages to the worker
1	Greater efficiency because workers practise their tasks repeatedly and become experts.	Workers become experts and can find employment more easily.
2	Greater use of specialist tools and equipment which improves efficiency.	Higher rates of pay can be earned if workers are experts.
3	Production time is reduced because workers do not have to move from one task to another.	People may become more skilled and enjoy a higher status at work.
4	Organisation is easier because each worker fits into a structured production process.	People may experience more job satisfaction and may have better promotion prospects.

Figure 13.1 *Advantages of the division of labour to firms and the worker.*

The disadvantages of the division of labour to the firm and the worker

	Disadvantages to the firm	Disadvantages to the worker
1	Productivity and quality might fall if tasks are too boring and repetitive.	People can become demoralised through repeating tasks and may lose interest in their work.
2	A lack of flexibility might exist if workers cannot be switched between jobs.	Unemployment if a specialist skill is no longer required because demand has fallen.
3	If a specialist is absent and can't be replaced the whole production process may halt.	Unemployment if repetitive tasks are taken over by machines.

Figure 13.2 *Disadvantages of the division of labour to firms and the worker.*

With the aid of an example, explain what is meant by the term division of labour. *(3)*

© Edexcel Question paper, January 2012

> The production process is often broken down into small parts and each worker is allocated a specific task. This is called the division of labour and it can help to improve productivity in business. For example on an assembly line in a car factory, tasks might include engine installation, brake installation, wheel installation and many other different assembly tasks.

TOP TIP

In this answer, 2 marks are awarded for giving a correct definition and 1 mark is awarded for describing a relevant example.

1 State **two** possible advantages of the division of labour for workers. *(2)*

2 Do the advantages of the division of labour always outweigh the disadvantages for a firm? Explain your answer. *(6)*

Chapter 14: **The labour market**

Wage determination

- The **wage rate** in a labour market is determined by the interaction of the supply and demand for labour.
- The equilibrium wage is determined where the supply and the demand for labour are equal. In Figure 14.1, this is US$15 per hour.

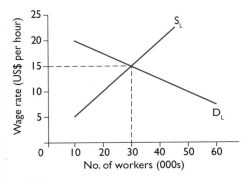

Figure 14.1 *Wage determination in a labour market.*

Factors affecting the demand for labour

- **The demand for the goods** produced by a particular firm.
- **The cost and availability of substitutes** If machines are cheaper than workers, firms may switch to using more machines.
- **Labour productivity** If workers can produce more output, the demand for labour increases.
- **Other employment costs** such as employment tax, recruitment costs, employee pensions and other perks.

Factors affecting the supply of labour

- **Changes in the school leaving age or the retirement age** If the school leaving age falls or the retirement age rises, the labour supply will rise.
- **The role of females in society** More females are abandoning the traditional roles of housekeeping and child rearing. Instead, they choose to work which increases the working population.
- **Net migration** Immigrants will increase the working population when they arrive from abroad. However, if emigration rises the working population will fall.

> The supply curve for labour is upward sloping because as the wage rate rises, an increasing number of people are prepared to work. Work is more worthwhile at higher wage rates.

Wage differences between different occupations

- The more skill, training or qualifications a job requires, the higher the wages.
- Wages will be higher for dangerous or dirty work, such as bomb disposal or sewerage management.

- In expanding industries, wages are forced up because the demand for labour is rising. The opposite happens in declining industries.
- Workers in trade unions may receive higher wages than those who are not members of trade unions.

Quality of labour–qualifications and training

- Firms want people who are literate, numerate and good communicators. Productivity will be higher if workers are well-educated and trained.
- The quality of **human capital** can be improved with investment in training and education. This responsibility is often shared between the state and firms.

The effect on wages of changes in the supply and demand for nurses

Figure 14.2 shows the effect on nurses' wages of: **1.** An ageing population, **2.** An increase in the retirement age, **3.** A rise in employment tax.

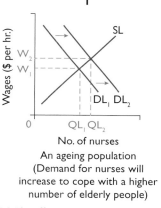

An ageing population
(Demand for nurses will increase to cope with a higher number of elderly people)

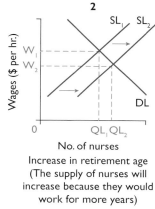

Increase in retirement age
(The supply of nurses will increase because they would work for more years)

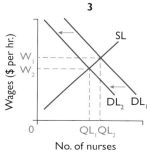

Rise in employment tax
(Demand for nurses will fall because it would be more expensive to employ them)

Figure 14.2 *The effect on wages of changes in the supply and demand for nurses.*

Worked Example

Which of the following will improve the quality of the working population?

    A Higher employment tax

    B Investment in education

    C Higher wages

    D Less training   *(1)*

B is the correct answer. Investment in education will help to improve literacy, numeracy and communication skills.

TOP TIP

When answering multiple choice questions make sure you read **ALL** the responses before choosing your answer.

Revision Questions

In 2010, 500,000 people were employed in the Canadian petroleum industry. This is expected to rise by about 10 per cent in the next five to 10 years as the demand for energy increases.

1 Why is the demand for petroleum workers likely to rise in Canada? *(3)*

2 Draw a supply and demand diagram to show the likely effect on the wages of petroleum workers of an increase in the demand for energy. *(4)*

3 Explain **two** factors that might affect the supply of petroleum workers in Canada. *(4)*

Chapter 15: **Interference in the labour market**

Minimum wage legislation

- Governments may interfere in the labour market by setting a minimum wage.
- This involves passing legislation which prevents employers from paying their workers an hourly rate less than a certain limit.

From January 1 2012, the minimum wage in the United States is US$7.25 per hour.

Reasons for minimum wage legislation

- **To benefit disadvantaged workers** People such as women and low-income families may be better off on the minimum wage.
- **To reduce poverty** Poor families often rely on earnings from low-paying jobs. A minimum wage reduces poverty, because these families receive more money.
- **To help businesses** A minimum wage should promote greater equality and fairness among workers. Therefore worker motivation will improve.

Effects of minimum wage legislation on wages and employment

- A minimum wage is set above the equilibrium wage.
- In Figure 15.1, the minimum wage is £7 per hour (above the equilibrium of £6 per hour).
- A minimum wage will reduce employment from 150,000 to 125,000. This is because fewer workers are demanded at the higher wage rate.
- Total unemployment at the minimum wage level will be 50,000 workers in this case.

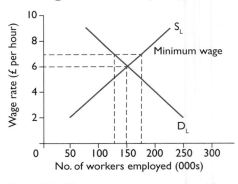

Figure 15.1 *Effects of a minimum wage in a labour market.*

Trade unions

Trade unions (TUs) are organisations that protect the interests of workers. They:

- negotiate pay and working conditions with employers;
- provide legal protection, for example representing workers in court;
- pressurise governments to pass legislation that improves workers' rights;
- provide benefits such as strike pay and other payments or benefits.

Effects of strong trade unions on wages and employment

- Strong TUs may force up wages.

- Trade unions can apply pressure on employers by threatening industrial action if their wage demands are not met.

- Employers may give in to trade unions to avoid disruption to their businesses.

- By forcing up wages, trade unions may also cause unemployment amongst their members. This is because employers may reduce demand for workers at the higher wage level.

> Job losses might be avoided when TUs drive up wages if labour productivity rises, if employers charge customers more or cut their profit margins.

Worked Example

In an attempt to improve the standard of living in the agricultural industry, a government introduces a minimum wage rate. On the diagram below, show the effect of the introduction of this minimum wage rate on wages and employment in the industry. *(4)*

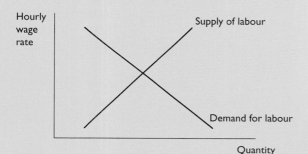

Figure 15.2 *Agricultural industry labour market.*

© *Edexcel Question paper, May 2012*

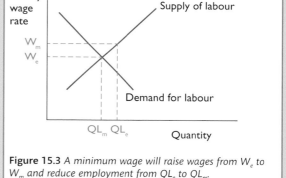

Figure 15.3 *A minimum wage will raise wages from W_e to W_m and reduce employment from QL_e to QL_m.*

TOP TIP ✓

Remember that a minimum wage is **always** set above the equilibrium wage.

Revision Questions

1 Introducing a minimum wage will:

    A   reduce the quality of labour

    B   reduce inflation

    C   increase pay for some workers

    D   not affect pay levels   *(1)*

2 State **two** reasons for introducing a minimum wage. *(2)*

3 How far is it possible for trade unions to increase wages and protect the employment of their members? Give reasons for your answer. *(6)*

PART 1 Production

Chapter 16: **The factors of production and productivity**

What is production?

Production is a process which involves converting resources into goods or services. Examples might include:

- a builder using glass, timber and other materials to construct a house,

- a gardener using a lawnmower, tools and implements to maintain a garden.

The four factors of production

These are the resources that are used in production.

Land

Land has two meanings in economics:

1. a 'plot of land' where businesses locate their premises

2. natural resources.

> Natural resources may be non-renewable such as coal, oil, diamonds and limestone (once they have been used they cannot be replaced). Or renewable resources such as fish, forests (replaced by farming and cultivation) and water (replaced by nature).

Labour

- **Labour** is the workforce in the economy. Manual workers, skilled workers and managers are all members of a nation's workforce.

- The value of an individual worker to a business is their **human capital**. This can be increased through training and education.

Capital

Capital is used in production to make goods and services. Two types exist:

- **working capital** such as stocks of raw materials and finished goods,

- **fixed capital** such as factories, shops, machines, tools and equipment.

Enterprise

Entrepreneurs set up and run businesses. Their role is summarised in Figure 16.1.

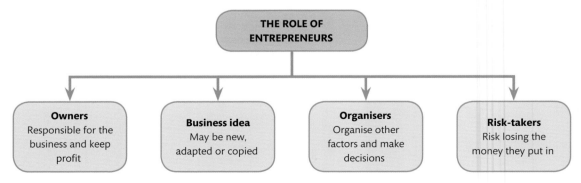

Figure 16.1 *The role of entrepreneurs.*

Labour intensive and capital intensive production

- **Labour intensive** production involves using relatively more labour than capital. The provision of services is usually labour intensive.

- **Capital intensive** production involves using relatively more capital than labour. In some countries, manufacturing often relies greatly on machinery.

Increasing production

- If the economy produces more goods and services, more factors of production will be needed.

- For example a farmer may acquire more land to increase wheat production, or a computer manufacturer may employ more staff to increase output.

Productivity

- Production can be increased by raising **productivity**. This involves using factors more effectively.

- Productivity is the output per unit of input. For example the productivity of labour is the output per worker. Labour productivity is discussed in more detail in Chapter 20.

- Firms try to increase productivity to lower costs and increase profit. They may do this by introducing new working practices or investing in new machinery.

Worked Example

Julia is a hairdresser. She used to work in a hairdressing salon but now she visits her clients in their homes.

Julia is an entrepreneur. Define the term *entrepreneur*.   (2)

© Edexcel Question paper, January 2012

> An entrepreneur is a person who sets up and runs a business. Entrepreneurs think of a business idea, hire and organise other factors of production and risk their money in the hope that the business makes a profit.

TOP TIP
Marks are often lost because definitions are too vague. Make sure that your definitions are clear and exact.

Revision Questions

1 Which of the following is **NOT** a factor of production?

    A Profit

    B Labour

    C Enterprise

    D Capital   (1)

2 With the aid of an example, explain what is meant by working capital.   (3)

3 What is the difference between production and productivity?   (4)

Chapter 17: **Sectors of the economy**

Primary sector

Production in the **primary sector** involves extracting raw materials from the earth.

- **Mining and quarrying** Raw materials such as coal, copper, gravel, diamonds, uranium, salt and limestone are dug from the ground.
- **Fishing** This is catching fish or gathering other types of seafood such as mussels, prawns, lobsters and oysters.
- **Forestry** This industry's activity is managing forests to provide timber and protecting the natural environment. For example providing public access and managing wildlife habitats.
- **Agriculture** This industry is producing foods, fibres, biofuels and ornamental products, such as flowers and birds for the pet trade.

Secondary sector

Production in the **secondary sector** involves converting raw materials into finished or semi-finished goods. Common examples of industries in this sector include:

- Manufacturing
- Processing
- Construction

Tertiary sector

The **tertiary sector** involves providing services such as the examples in Figure 17.1.

Service	Examples
Professional	Accountancy, Legal advice, Teaching
Household	Decorating, Gardening, Appliance repairs
Transport	Train, Taxi, Bus, Air
Leisure	Tourism, Restaurants, Sport, Cinema
Financial	Banking, Insurance, Pensions, Advisory
Commercial	Cleaning, Printing, Logistics, IT, Marketing

Figure 17.1 *Examples of tertiary sector production.*

Changes in employment and output over time

- Different sectors grow and decline over time.
- In the United Kingdom, before the Industrial Revolution began in the late 18th century, most employment was in the primary sector.
- In the 19th century, secondary production expanded due to the Industrial Revolution.
- In the last 60 years, the tertiary sector has expanded at the expense of manufacturing. Possible reasons for this are summarised in Figure 17.2.

The growth in the tertiary sector at the expense of manufacturing is called **de-industrialisation**.

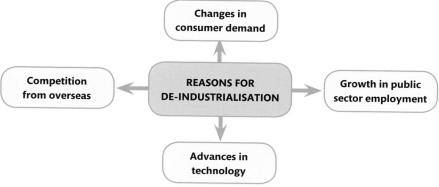

Figure 17.2 *Possible reasons for de-industrialisation.*

Developed and developing countries

Changes in the structures of both developed and developing economies have taken place in recent decades. However, not all countries follow these patterns.

Developed countries

- Sharply decreasing primary sector production
- Decreasing manufacturing
- Rapidly growing tertiary sector

Developing countries

- Declining primary sector production
- Increasing manufacturing
- Some growth in the tertiary sector

Revision Questions

Many developing nations are beginning to enjoy higher levels of growth in their economies. The graph in Figure 17.3 compares the contributions made by services and manufacturing in developed and developing countries.

1 What is meant by the *tertiary sector*? **(2)**

2 Which of these is an example of production in the primary sector?

    A Canning and bottling
    B Beekeeping
    C Accountancy
    D Motorway construction   **(1)**

3 Look at Figure 17.3. Discuss **two** reasons for the size of the contribution made by manufacturing to growth in developed and developing countries. **(4)**

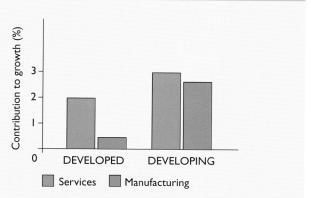

Figure 17.3 *Sources of growth in developed and developing countries (1980–2009).*

Chapter 18: **Production costs and revenue**

Fixed costs and variable costs

Cost	Definition	Examples
Fixed (FC)	Remain unchanged at all levels of output	Rent, rates and interest
Variable (VC)	Change when output changes, for example they rise when output rises	Materials, packaging and fuel

Figure 18.1 *Fixed costs and variable costs.*

Total costs and average costs

Cost	Definition	Formula
Total (TC)	All of the costs of production over a period of time	TC = FC + VC
Average (AC)	Sometimes called unit cost—the cost of producing a single unit	AC = TC ÷ Q

Figure 18.2 *Total costs and average costs (NB Q = output).*

The average cost curve

The average cost curve is U-shaped because as output (Q) increases, average costs fall at first, reach a minimum and then start to rise. In Figure 18.3:

- When Q = 1000 units, AC = US$30.

- When Q rises to 3000 units, AC = US$18. This is the minimum average cost in this example.

- When Q rises further to 4500 units, AC = US$25.

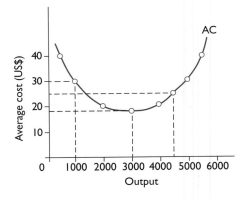

Figure 18.3 *An average cost curve.*

The main reason why the average cost curve is U-shaped is explained more fully in Chapter 19.

Price and total revenue

Price is the amount of money customers pay for a product. The money that a firm receives from selling products is its **total revenue**.

Total revenue = Price × Quantity (TR = P × Q)

Profit and loss

The difference between total revenue and total costs is **profit** or **loss**.

Profit (Loss) = Total revenue – Total cost

(Profit (Loss) = TR – TC)

Calculating costs, revenue and profit—an example

A manufacturer makes plastic dustbins for garbage collectors. Production costs are shown in Figure 18.4.

Wages	US$1.00 per bin
Raw materials	US$2.40 per bin
Other variable costs	US$1.60 per bin
Rent and rates	US$100,000 per annum
Other fixed costs	US$80,000 per annum

Figure 18.4 *Production costs for a dustbin manufacturer.*

In 2012, 50,000 bins were produced—costs were:

FC = **US$180,000** (US$100,000 + US$80,000)
VC = **US$250,000** {50,000 × (US$1.00 + US$2.40 + US$1.60)}
TC = FC + VC = US$180,000 + US$250,000 = **US$430,000**

If the dustbins are sold for US$10:

TR = US$10 × 50,000 = **US$500,000**
Profit = TR − TC = US$500,000 − US$430,000 = **US$70,000**

Worked Example

Julia is a hairdresser. She used to work in a hairdressing salon but now she visits clients in their homes.

Below is a list of some of Julia's costs. Place each cost in the correct column. **(3)**

Example: Loan repayments are fixed costs.
1. Petrol
2. Car insurance
3. Shampoo

Fixed costs	Variable costs
Loan repayments	

Fixed costs	Variable costs
Loan repayments	Petrol
Car insurance	Shampoo

© *Edexcel Question paper, January 2012*

TOP TIP

The aim of this example is not to test the mathematical ability of candidates. Questions relating to costs, revenue and profit will only require simple numerical calculations.

Revision Questions

An ice-cream seller rents an ice-cream van for US$500 per week and has no other fixed costs. One summer week, sales were 2,000 ice creams. Variable costs were US$0.50 per ice cream and ice creams sold for US$1 each.

1 Define the term *fixed cost*. **(2)**

2 For the summer week calculate:
   (i) Total costs **(2)**
   (ii) Total revenue **(2)**
   (iii) Profit **(2)**

3 Calculate the effect on profit if the seller raises price to US$1.50 and sales fall to 1,200 ice creams? **(3)**

Chapter 19: Economies and diseconomies of scale

Economies of scale

- Big firms can produce goods more cheaply than small firms can because as firms begin to expand, average costs (AC) start to fall.
- This is due to **economies of scale** as shown in Figure 19.1.
- When output = 10,000, AC = US$2.50.
- If output is doubled to 20,000 units, AC falls to US$1.50.
- AC continues to fall until output = 30,000. Here, AC is minimised at US$1.20.

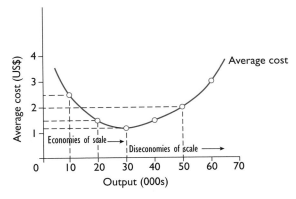

Figure 19.1 *Economies and diseconomies of scale.*

The long-run average cost curve is U-shaped due to economies and diseconomies of scale.

Internal economies of scale

Internal economies of scale are the cost benefits enjoyed by a single firm when it expands. Examples of benefits are shown in Figure 19.2.

Economy	Examples of benefits to large firms
Purchasing	Discounts when bulk buying raw materials and other resources
Marketing	Fixed marketing costs such as a TV advert can be spread over more units of output
Technical	Large factories are more efficient, and there can be more specialisation
Financial	More sources to choose from and lower rates of interest from banks
Managerial	Specialists such as accountants can be employed to improve efficiency
Risk-bearing	Wider product ranges and more markets help to reduce business risk

Figure 19.2 *Examples of internal economies of scale.*

External economies of scale

If an industry is concentrated in a particular region, firms may enjoy **external economies of scale**, that is falling ACs for all firms in the industry.

```
              ┌─────────────────────────────┐
              │   EXAMPLES OF EXTERNAL      │
              │   ECONOMIES OF SCALE        │
              └─────────────────────────────┘
```

Skilled labour	Infrastructure	Commercial services	Cooperation
There may be a build up of labour which has the skills and work experience needed by that industry. This helps to cut training costs.	Roads, railways, airports and business parks, for example, will be shaped to suit the needs of the dominant industry.	Specialist suppliers such as marketing, cleaning, banking, insurance and waste disposal will be attracted to the area.	When firms in the same industry are located close to each other they may cooperate more by sharing an R & D centre for example.

Figure 19.3 *Examples of external economies of scale.*

Diseconomies of scale

In Figure 19.1, if the firm expands beyond 30,000 units, average costs (AC) start to rise. For example if the firm produces 50,000 units, AC rises to US$2.00 per unit. This is because of **diseconomies of scale**. AC rises because inefficiencies occur. Causes may be:

- **Bureaucracy** Large firms may become more bureaucratic. For example they may require extra form-filling and report writing. Decision-making and communication may also become slower.

- **Labour relations** Relations between workers and managers may worsen. The needs of individual workers may be neglected and their motivation may suffer.

- **Control and coordination** Large firms with thousands of employees and dozens of factories all over the world may be difficult to keep under control and coordinate.

Worked Example

Which of the following costs fall as a result of economies of scale? *(1)*

A Total cost

B Fixed cost

C Variable cost

D Average cost

D is the correct answer. It is average costs that are influenced by both economies and diseconomies of scale.

TOP TIP

It is important to understand the differences between the costs listed. Remember, when discussing economies of scale it is always about average (or unit) costs.

Revision Questions

Walmart is the largest US general retailer. The firm can buy in bulk such huge quantities that their suppliers are forced to offer discounts. This means that Walmart can offers its customers lower prices.

1 Using the example above, explain what is meant by *internal economies of scale*. (2)

2 Define *diseconomies of scale*. (2)

3 To what extent might consumers benefit from *economies of scale*? (6)

Chapter 20: **Productivity and wealth creation**

Productivity and wealth creation

- A nation's wealth can be increased by improving its productivity.

- Figure 20.1 shows that increased productivity will shift the PPC out to the right from PPC_1 to PPC_2.

- This means the economy can produce more of both capital goods and consumer goods with its limited resources.

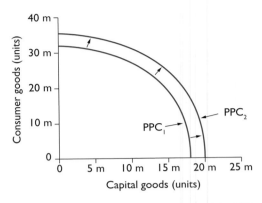

Figure 20.1 *Improvements in productivity and the PPC.*

Improving the productivity of land

Some land is fertile and can be used to grow food, but some is infertile and almost useless. However, land can be made more productive. For example:

- Fertilisers and pesticides can raise crop yields.

- Irrigation can divert the water in rivers or lakes to unproductive land.

- Flooded land, such as swampland, can be drained and then farmed.

- Disease-resistant and higher-yielding genetically modified (GM) crops can be grown.

> There is some resistance to the use of GM crops because genetic engineering is imprecise and unpredictable. GM crops may have unknown adverse health effects.

Labour productivity

Labour productivity is defined as output per worker. It can be calculated as:

$$\text{Labour productivity} = \frac{\text{Total output}}{\text{No. of workers}}$$

For example a tractor manufacturer, employing 200 workers produces 4,000 tractors in 2012.

$$\text{Labour productivity} = 4,000 \div 200$$
$$= 20 \text{ tractors per worker}$$

Improving labour productivity

If the quality of human capital can be improved labour productivity will rise. Measures which could be used to improve labour productivity include:

- **Education and training** Government investment in education and business investment in training

- **Improve the motivation of workers** Financial incentive schemes such as piece rates or non-financial methods such as job rotation and team working

- **Improve working practices** Changing factory layout to improve the flow of production or making labour more flexible.

Improving capital productivity

The introduction of new technology can improve capital productivity in all three sectors of the economy.

```
                    ┌─────────────────────────┐
                    │  IMPROVING CAPITAL      │
                    │  PRODUCTIVITY           │
                    └─────────────────────────┘
```

PRIMARY SECTOR
In agriculture machinery, irrigation, the computerised tracking of livestock, fertilisers and pesticides have helped to increase output.

SECONDARY SECTOR
Flow production, robots, computer numerically controlled machines and computer-integrated manufacturing are used to raise output.

TERTIARY SECTOR
Online shopping has improved productivity in retailing and banking. Dramatic advances in medicine and surgical technology have raised productivity in healthcare.

Figure 20.2 *Improving capital productivity.*

PART 1 Chapter 20: Productivity and wealth creation

Worked Example

It is easier for firms in the secondary sector to increase the productivity of labour than it is for firms in the primary sector. Do you agree with this statement? Justify your answer. **(6)**

© *Edexcel Question paper, May 2012*

In the secondary sector, labour productivity might be increased by introducing financial-incentive schemes. For example, a piece rate rewards workers for higher levels of output. If workers are motivated by money, such a method might improve labour productivity. In the primary sector, labour productivity may be increased by making use of fertilisers or pesticides. These could help to increase crop yields. It could be argued that the statement is incorrect. This is because the primary sector often has access to the same methods as the secondary sector has. For example financial-incentive schemes could be used in both sectors to motivate workers.

TOP TIP ✓

Two marks are awarded for identifying and explaining a method in the secondary sector, 2 marks for doing the same thing in the primary sector and a further 2 marks for evaluation. There is no wrong or right answer to this type of question. It could also be argued that the statement is correct, because increasing productivity in the primary sector may be limited due to factors outside the control of man, for example the weather.

Revision Questions

1   Define *labour productivity*. **(2)**

2   A motorcycle factory produced 24,000 motor cycles in 2012. Calculate labour productivity if 600 workers were employed. **(3)**

3   Explain how rising productivity can affect the wealth of a nation. **(4)**

Chapter 21: Externalities: costs and benefits

Social cost

The production or consumption of a good has costs.

| SOCIAL COST
The costs to society as a whole of an economic activity | = | PRIVATE COST
Costs that are met by those who produce or consume a good | + | NEGATIVE EXTERNALITIES
Costs that are not met by those who impose them |

Figure 21.1 *Social cost.*

Social benefit

The production or consumption of a good also has benefits.

| SOCIAL BENEFIT
The benefits to society as a whole of an economic activity | = | PRIVATE BENEFIT
Benefits enjoyed by those who produce or consume a good | + | POSITIVE EXTERNALITIES
Benefits enjoyed by third parties |

Figure 21.2 *Social benefit.*

Examples of externalities in production

Externalities are the 'spillover' effects of production. They can be positive or negative.

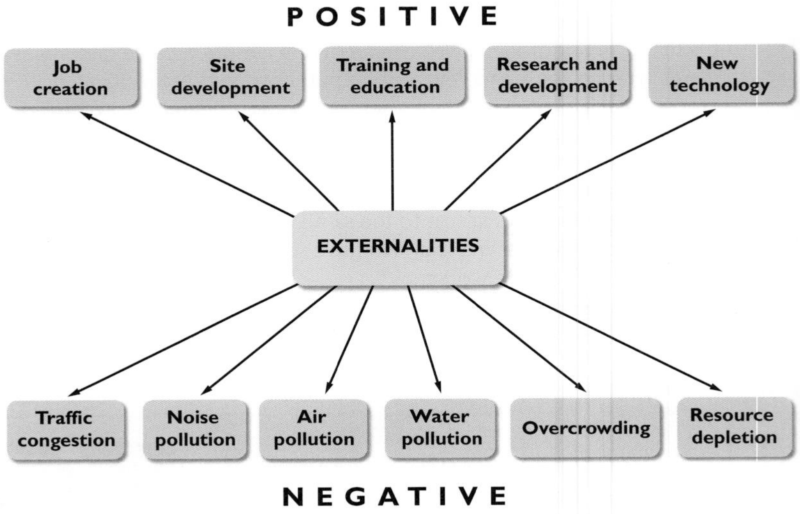

POSITIVE

Job creation · Site development · Training and education · Research and development · New technology

EXTERNALITIES

Traffic congestion · Noise pollution · Air pollution · Water pollution · Overcrowding · Resource depletion

NEGATIVE

Figure 21.3 *Examples of externalities in production.*

An example of externalities in consumption

Consider a person who buys a remote-controlled model aircraft.

- Private cost = US$239 + running costs
- External cost = the noise pollution resulting from its operation in a public place (when flying, model planes can make a loud screeching noise)
- Private benefit = the pleasure the owner has from flying it
- External benefit = the possible pleasure onlookers have when the owner flies it in a public space

Government policies to deal with externalities

Governments try to reduce externalities because they often result in high costs. For example global warming might have very serious and expensive consequences if left unchecked. Government policies might include:

- **Taxation** Pollution may be reduced if a tax is imposed on firms producing harmful waste. This will raise costs, increase prices and cut demand.

- **Subsidies** Subsidies may be given to those that generate positive externalities. For example grants may be made to people who install solar panels to generate clean electricity.

- **Fines** Financial penalties may be given to those who damage the environment. For example there may be fines for firms that pollute the waterways or the atmosphere.

- **Government regulation** The EU's Emissions Trading Directive limits the amount of carbon dioxide that firms can release into the atmosphere.

- **Other measures** For example there are congestion charges and international agreements such as The Kyoto Protocol which set targets to reduce global pollution.

Worked Example

Cars produce negative externalities.
(a) Identify **one** negative externality produced by cars. *(1)*
(b) Briefly explain **one** reason why governments try to reduce negative externalities produced by cars. *(2)*

© *Edexcel Question paper, June 2011*

> (a) Air pollution
> (b) Serious air pollution can cause health problems such as respiratory illnesses. This could result in higher government expenditure in the health service.

TOP TIP

When answering this question a lot of candidates listed more than one reason why governments try to reduce negative externalities, rather than explaining just one. This shows that it is important to read the question carefully and answer it as instructed.

Revision Questions

1 What is the difference between social cost and private cost? *(2)*

2 State **two** methods that a government could use to reduce the negative externalities illustrated in the photograph. *(2)*

3 With reference to both methods identified in your answer to question 2, which one is likely to be better at reducing negative externalities? *(6)*

Air pollution

PART 2 Competition

Chapter 22: **Competitive markets**

What is a competitive market?

- The rivalry between firms trying to sell goods in a market is called **competition**.

- In a competitive market there are lots of sellers, prices are very similar and their products can be easily substituted for one another.

- It is easy to break into the market because there are no **barriers to entry**.

> There are 15,000 milk producers in the United Kingdom. The milk sold by each producer is almost identical and the price they receive for their output is the same. This is a competitive market.

Competition and the firm

Firms do not welcome competition. They would prefer to dominate the market and operate without the threat of rivals. To survive firms must:

- Minimise their costs by operating efficiently

- Provide good quality products

- Charge fair prices

- Innovate by constantly reviewing and improving products.

Disadvantage to firms in a competitive market is that profit is limited. The total profit in the industry has to be shared between many firms.

Advantage to firms that flourish in competitive markets is that they will be efficient and have greater ability to compete in overseas markets.

Competition and the consumer

Advantages	
Lower prices	Goods are close substitutes, therefore consumers can easily switch to a cheaper rival.
More choice	The high number of firms are pressed to innovate and make their products different.
Better quality	Poor quality goods will not be bought by consumers—they will switch to rival goods.
Disadvantages	
Uncertainty	Frequent entry and exit of firms may disrupt the market and cause confusion.
Less innovation	Lower profit levels leave fewer resources available for Research and Development and innovation.

Figure 22.1 *Advantages and disadvantages to consumers of competitive markets.*

Competition and the economy

Advantages of competitive markets:

- Resources are allocated more effectively. This is because firms have to operate efficiently to survive. They are under pressure to minimise costs.

- There is more innovation due to the competitive pressure on firms. Innovation will benefit the economy, since living standards will be higher.

Disadvantage of competitive markets:

- Resources might be wasted because some production factors are immobile. When firms close down it takes time for resources to transfer to other uses. This can be wasteful.

Worked Example

Which of the following is a benefit to an **economy** with a competitive market?

A   More product choice

B   High prices

C   Resources are allocated more effectively

D   There are barriers to entry   *(1)*

C is the correct answer. Resources are allocated more effectively. This is because firms have to operate efficiently to survive. They are under pressure to minimise costs.

TOP TIP
It is very important to understand what is meant by competition. It is a key concept in economics and will feature in other chapters.

Revision Questions

A competitive market

1   Use the example in the photograph to explain what is meant by a competitive market?   *(3)*

2   Competitive markets have no barriers to entry. Explain what this means.   *(3)*

3   Explain **two** reasons why consumers benefit from a competitive market.   *(4)*

Chapter 23: **Advantages and disadvantages of large and small firms**

How is the size of a firm measured?

- **Turnover** The revenue a firm receives from selling output
- **Number of employees** The number of people who are employed
- **Capital employed** The amount of money invested in the business

Small firms

In most economies, the majority of firms are small. For example in India there are nearly 30 million small businesses. In the United Kingdom, about 99 per cent of all firms are small.

Advantages	Explanation
Flexibility	They can adapt to change more quickly because the owners (decision-makers) are actively involved in the business.
Personal service	They can offer a personal service because the owners are more accessible to the customer.
Lower wages	Employees are less likely to belong to trade unions and therefore they have less negotiating power.
Better communications	With fewer employees, communication is more effective and the owner is more in touch with the staff.
Innovation	They are often under pressure to innovate in order to survive in the market.

Figure 23.1 *Advantages enjoyed by small firms.*

Disadvantages	Explanation
Higher costs	They cannot exploit economies of scale and so unit costs are higher than those of larger rival firms.
Lack of finance	They struggle to raise finance because lenders consider small firms too risky. Their choice of sources of finance is also limited.
Recruitment problems	They may lack the resources to attract the best staff available.
Vulnerable	When trading conditions deteriorate, they may struggle because they lack the resources needed to survive.

Figure 23.2 *Disadvantages faced by small firms.*

Large firms

- In most economies only a small percentage of firms are large. However, this minority of large firms generally contributes nearly half of all business turnover.
- Large firms are more powerful than smaller rival firms are.

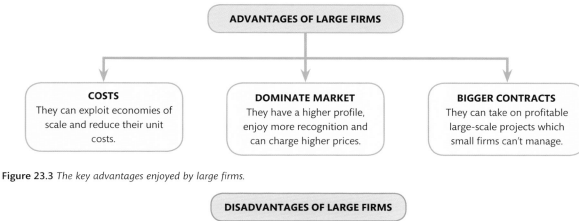

Figure 23.3 *The key advantages enjoyed by large firms.*

Figure 23.4 *The key disadvantages faced by large firms.*

Worked Example

Since 2006, BizziBus, a Sydney-based bus company has increasd its turnover from AU\$1.2m to AU\$78.4m. It is now nationally recognised and runs services all over Australia.

1 To what extent do the advantages of being a large company outweigh the disadvantages? **(6)**

> Large firms can take advantage of economies of scale, which means that their unit costs are lower. This can result in higher profit. Large firms can also dominate the market because they have a higher profile. For example, BizziBus is now recognised nationally in Australia. However, large firms might encounter diseconomies of scale. They may be overwhelmed with administration and may thus lose control of their operations. Also, workers may suffer from poor motivation. As a result, costs may rise. It could be argued that the advantages outweigh the disadvantages because firms can take measures to deal with problems, such as poor motivation, by offering their workers financial or non-financial incentives.

TOP TIP

Two marks are awarded for identifying and explaining an advantage, 2 marks for doing the same for a disadvantage and a further 2 marks for evaluation. You can evaluate by giving good reasons for the judgement that you have made.

Revision Questions

1 State **two** ways in which the size of a firm can be measured. **(2)**

2 Why might small firms struggle to raise finance? **(2)**

3 Explain **two** advantages to firms of remaining small. **(4)**

Chapter 24: **The growth of firms**

Motives for growth

- **Survival** Large firms can deal better with competition and poor trading conditions because they have more resources.

- **Economies of scale** Large firms can enjoy lower average costs when they exploit economies of scale. This improves efficiency and profitability.

- **Increase profits** Large firms generate more revenue and profit because they have big market shares and more products in more markets.

- **Increase market share** With a larger market share, firms can charge more, enjoy a higher profile and establish its brand more effectively.

- **Reduce risk** Branching out into new markets and new products means that if one product fails, success in others can keep the firm going.

Methods of growth

- Internal growth or **organic growth** involves a firm increasing its output and selling more in its existing market or in new markets.

- External growth is faster and involves joining with another firm through a **takeover** or a **merger**.

- Figure 24.1 shows the different types of integration.

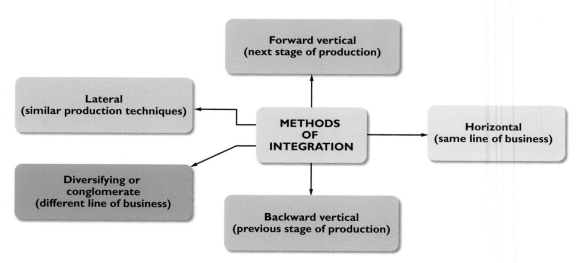

Figure 24.1 *Methods of integration.*

Limitations to growth

Sometimes obstacles prevent growth. For example:

- **Limited market** Small markets may be unsuitable for large firms. For example a village shop cannot grow easily because the customer base is small.

- **Lack of finance (capital)** Small businesses struggle to obtain the finance that they need to grow. Lenders consider them too risky.

- **Aim of the entrepreneur** Some owners prefer to remain small to avoid VAT registration or the responsibility of running a larger business.

- **Low barriers to entry** In some markets the set-up costs are low, so fierce competition stops any individual firm from growing.

- **Diseconomies of scale** A firm is not likely to grow any further if its costs start to rise because it starts to lose its competitiveness.

Worked Example

Alan Wong is a taxi driver. Like many other taxi drivers in his city, he owns his taxi and runs his own business.

1 *(a)* One reason why firms such as Alan's may remain small is:

    A economies of scale

    B horizontal integration

    C technological economies

    D lack of capital   *(1)*

(b) Explain why you chose your answer in (a).   *(2)*

© Edexcel Sample Assessment Material

(a)   **D** is the correct answer.

(b)   Extra capital is usually needed to pay for the resources that are required for a business to grow. Small businesses often struggle to obtain this finance. Lenders consider small business as high risk. They think that small businesses may struggle to pay the interest and to repay the amount they borrowed.

TOP TIP

Remember that since 2008, in many countries, there has been a 'credit crunch'. This means that banks have been unwilling to lend. Small businesses have found it particularly difficult to raise finance.

Revision Questions

In 2012, Ecobank Ghana Ltd merged with The Trust Bank Ltd (TTB), also of Ghana. The Managing Director of Ecobank, said that the merger was a strategic move by the bank to consolidate its leadership position in the Ghanaian banking industry.

1 The merger described above is an example of a horizontal merger. What does this mean?   *(2)*

2 Explain **two** possible reasons why the banking merger took place.   *(4)*

3 To what extent is the growth of firms limited? Give reasons for your answer.   *(6)*

Chapter 25: **Monopoly**

What is monopoly?

- A monopoly exists when a single firm dominates a market.

- A **pure monopoly** exists when a market is supplied by one producer.

- In some countries, a **legal monopoly** may be when one firm has 25 per cent or more of a market.

> Pure monopolies are not common but they do exist. For example in some countries pure monopolists operate in the water and rail industries.

Features of monopoly

- **Barriers to entry** are a common feature in monopoly because they discourage competition. They are obstacles that prevent new firms from entering the market.

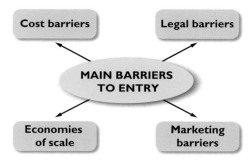

Figure 25.1 *The main barriers to entry.*

- **Unique product** The product supplied by a monopolist will be highly differentiated. There will not be another exactly like it.

- **Control over price** Monopolists force prices to rise by restricting supply. However, they cannot fix both price and supply. If they try to sell more, the price will be forced down.

The advantages of monopoly

Advantages	Explanation
More research & development	With their high profit levels, monopolies have the resources to invest in R & D and generate new products for consumers.
Lower costs	Large monopolists can exploit economies of scale. This reduces costs and might mean lower prices for consumers.
Natural monopolies	In some markets such as rail travel and water distribution, it is cost-effective to have one supplier. Wasteful duplication is avoided.
Internationally competitive	Successful monopolies can compete more easily overseas. This will create jobs and exports in the producing country.

Figure 25.2 *Possible advantages to consumers of monopolies' products.*

The disadvantages of monopoly

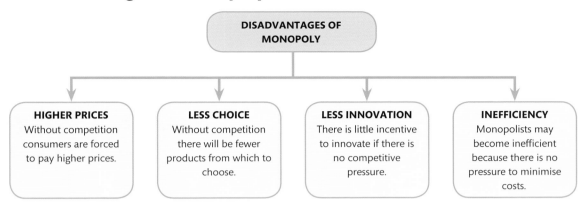

Figure 25.3 *Disadvantages of monopoly.*

Worked Example

Monopolies, such as Telcel, are always bad for consumers. Do you agree with this statement? Give reasons for your answer. *(6)*

© Edexcel Question paper, May 2012

> One advantage to consumers of monopolies is lower prices. Monopolists are usually large firms so they can exploit economies of scale. As a result, their costs will be lower and may be reflected in lower prices. However, in contrast, prices are likely to be higher. This is because monopolists do not have rivals, so consumers have to pay whatever monopolists charge or go without the product. There is no real incentive for monopolists to lower their prices. They can charge higher prices and enjoy higher profits. Monopolies could be good for consumers, provided that the government carefully monitors their activities. For example, they may enforce restrictions on price increases or try to encourage competition.

TOP TIP

One mark is awarded here for identifying an advantage and another for development. One mark is awarded for identifying a disadvantage and another for development. The other 2 marks are for a reasoned conclusion or judgement.

Revision Questions

1 Which of the following is a feature of monopoly?

   A Firms have no control over the price charged

   B The product sold by all firms in the market is exactly the same

   C Barriers to entry exist

   D A small number of firms dominate the market *(1)*

2 Explain how consumers might benefit from a natural monopoly in a market. *(3)*

3 Explain **two** barriers to entry that a monopolist may use. *(4)*

Chapter 26: **Oligopoly**

Features of oligopoly

An **oligopoly** is a market dominated by a few large firms.

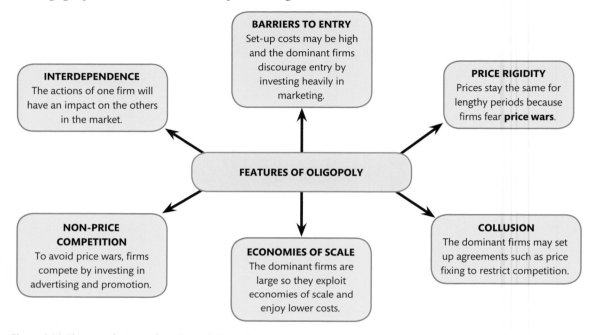

Figure 26.1 *The main features of an oligopolistic market.*

In many countries collusion is illegal because price agreements exploit consumers.

Advantages of oligopoly

Since there is some competition in oligopolistic markets consumers may benefit.

- **Economies of scale** If the dominant firms exploit economies of scale their costs will be lower which might mean lower prices for consumers.

- **Price stability** Stable prices will create some certainty in the market but consumers may also benefit from price wars if prices are cut aggressively.

- **Choice** Non-price competition can result in more choice for consumers, as firms continually launch new brands. Choice is also provided by the small producers that supply **niche markets**.

Price wars may not last for very long and there is the threat that one of the firms is squeezed out of the market. As a result, the market becomes less competitive and in the long term prices might rise even higher.

Disadvantages of oligopoly

- Firms may be tempted to collude about price. If firms fix prices, for example, consumers will pay more. If the market is shared out there will be less choice.

- A **cartel** might exist where a group of firms or countries join together and fix prices or output levels. If such cartels are successful, they act as a monopoly in the market. Cartels are illegal in most countries.

- The dominant firms spend huge amounts on advertising and promotion. Many consumers might prefer to have lower prices with less spent on advertising.

> One example of an international cartel is OPEC. Its members include some of the major oil-producing countries in world. Their aim is to restrict the supply of oil so that the price is forced up.

Worked Example

1. **(a)** Define the term *oligopoly*. **(2)**

   (b) Which of the following is **NOT** a possible feature of oligopoly? **(1)**

   - **A** Collusion
   - **B** Interdependence
   - **C** Non-price competition
   - **D** Low barriers to entry

   > 1. **(a)** An oligopoly exists where a market is dominated by a few large producers. Small producers may survive by supplying market niches but most of the industry's output is supplied by a few large firms.
   >
   >   **(b)** **D** is the correct answer. Barriers to entry are high in oligopolistic markets.

TOP TIP

Although an oligopolistic market is dominated by a few large producers, remember that small firms can survive by supplying a niche market.

PART 2 Chapter 26: Oligopoly

Revision Questions

Figure 26.2 shows the market shares of the world's main car producers.

1. What evidence is there in Figure 26.2 to support the view that the global car market is an oligopoly? **(2)**

2. Explain how consumers might benefit from an oligopolistic market. **(4)**

3. To what extent do you think barriers to entry exist in the car industry? **(6)**

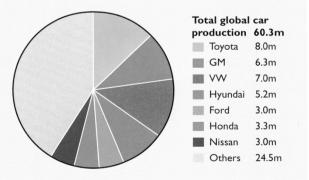

Total global car production	60.3m
Toyota	8.0m
GM	6.3m
VW	7.0m
Hyundai	5.2m
Ford	3.0m
Honda	3.3m
Nissan	3.0m
Others	24.5m

Figure 26.2 *Global car production 2010.*

PART 3 Public and private sectors

Chapter 27: **Public and private sectors**

Ownership and control in the public sector

The public sector includes organisations which are owned and controlled by local or central government. They are funded mainly from tax revenue. Some UK examples are shown in Figure 27.1.

Organisation	Ownership	Control	Examples
Central government departments	The state	Boards or teams led by a government minister	Ministry of Defence Department of Health
Local authority services	Local authorities	Councillors elected by local voters	Fire and police service, social services and recreation
Executive agencies	The state	Boards accountable to a central government department	Her Majesty's Prison Service, Court Service
Other organisations	The state	Boards or Trusts led by an experienced expert	BBC, Network Rail, Post Office, Bank of England

Figure 27.1 *Public sector organisations in the United Kingdom.*

> Governments also borrow money and make charges for some services such as issuing passports and administering driving tests.

Ownership and control in the private sector

- In the **private sector** goods and services are provided by businesses that are owned and controlled by individuals.

- There are different types of business organisations in the private sector. They vary according to legal ownership and size. However, in many countries, the majority of businesses are small or medium-sized enterprises.

- In many countries most consumer goods are provided by the private sector.

Private sector aims

Most private sector businesses aim to make a profit. However, Figure 27.2 shows that other aims exist.

Figure 27.2 *The aims of firms in the private sector.*

Public sector aims

- **Improve the quality of services** Performance indicators are used to monitor service quality. They focus on reliability, professionalism, levels of customer service and speed of service.

- **Minimise costs** Government resources are scarce, so it is important to minimise both waste and costs to reduce the burden on the taxpayer.

- **Allow for social costs and benefits** Since their aim is not to make a profit, public sector organisations may consider the needs of more stakeholders. For example they can take into account externalities.

Worked Example

Air India is owned by the Indian government. In recent years it has suffered from rising losses, discontented workers and falling market share on its domestic routes. Public limited companies such as IndiGo and SpiceJet are providing stiff competition.

Complete the sentences below from the following list.

Shareholders – public sector – the state – customers – make profits – taxation

1   *(a)* Air India is a .... business
      organisation.   *(1)*

    (b) Companies like IndiGo and SpiceJet are
      owned by ....   *(1)*

    (c) The main aim of a private sector
      business is to ....   *(1)*

---

1   *(a)* public sector
    (b) shareholders
    (c) make profits

TOP TIP

You need to recognise that the role of the public sector varies in different countries. For example in India, air transport is provided by both the private and the public sectors.

Revision Questions

1   Which **one** of the following is a possible aim of a private sector business?

    A   Growth

    B   Maximise employment

    C   Reduce inflation

    D   Lower interest rates   *(1)*

2   Explain how public sector organisations are funded.   *(4)*

3   Explain **two** aims of public sector organisations.   *(4)*

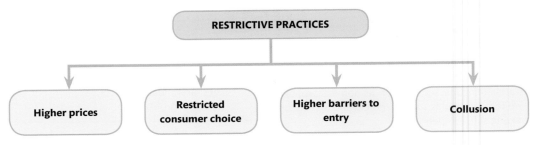

Chapter 28: **Government regulation**

The need for government regulation

There may be a need to control monopolies and merger activity. If a market is dominated by a one or a few very large firms, consumers may be exploited. Firms may use **restrictive practices** like those in Figure 28.1.

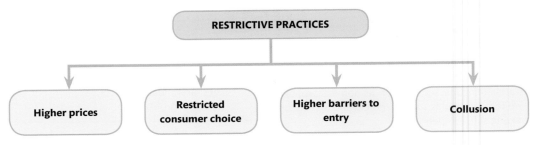

Figure 28.1 *Restrictive practices.*

How can a government promote competition?

- **Encourage the growth of small firms** If more small firms are encouraged to join markets there will be more competition.

- **Lower barriers to entry** If barriers are lowered or removed then more firms will join a market, thus making it more competitive.

- **Introduce anti-competitive legislation** Laws can be made to protect consumers from exploitation by firms.

> In the United Kingdom the Competition Commission (CC) investigates mergers and markets where consumers may be exploited. For example if it thinks that a merger will reduce competition, it can stop the merger or set conditions which must be met for the merger to go ahead.

Government influence in the location of firms

Regional policy can be used to encourage or discourage business location in particular areas. It is used to solve regional problems such as:

- **Unemployment** by providing jobs in areas which are in decline. Firms are offered incentives such as investment grants and tax advantages and are encouraged to locate in areas where unemployment is high.

- **Congestion** by reducing development in congested areas. Where there is traffic congestion and housing shortages, a heavy burden on public services such schools and hospitals already exists.

- **Income inequality** by encouraging firms to locate in poorer regions. In many countries, income levels are not constant across all regions.

Measures used to influence the location of firms

Financial incentives can influence the location of firms. These include:

- grants for investment
- money for training
- government investment in the infrastructure
- employment subsidies.

Congestion can be reduced by refusing planning permission for new developments in the congested areas.

Worked Example

Briefly explain **two** ways in which a government can promote competition in an economy. **(4)**

© Edexcel Sample Assessment Material

> One way to promote competition is to encourage the growth of small firms. If more small firms are encouraged to join markets, there will be more competition. Small firms could be encouraged to set up by offering them assistance such as free advice or help with funding.
>
> Another approach would be to introduce anti-competitive legislation. This involves passing laws that are designed to protect consumers from exploitation by firms, mergers and restrictive practices. Such laws would help to prevent dominant firms from reducing competition in markets.

TOP TIP

Make sure that you understand what is meant by competition in markets. It might be helpful to look back at Chapter 22.

Revision Questions

In 2009, the Polish Office of Competition and Consumer Protection fined seven large Polish cement producers a total of €100m. The companies had formed a cartel to fix prices and share the market over an 11 year period. The result of the formation of the cartel was to force up cement prices.

1. Using this case as an example, explain why government regulation is needed in business. **(4)**

2. State **two** reasons why a government should influence the location of firms. **(2)**

3. How important are government schemes in encouraging the setting up of small firms in an economy? **(6)**

Chapter 29: **Privatisation**

What is privatisation?

Privatisation is the transfer of public sector assets to the private sector. It involves:

- **Sale of nationalised industries** Nationalised industries are state-owned and state-run businesses. They are usually large and provide key services such as rail transport, electricity and water.
- **Deregulation** This involves lifting legal restrictions that prevent competition in the private sector.
- **Contracting out** Some government services such as cleaning, school meals and garbage collection have been 'contracted out' to the private sector.
- **The sale of land and property** For example tenants of council-owned properties are given the right to buy their houses.

The motives for privatisation

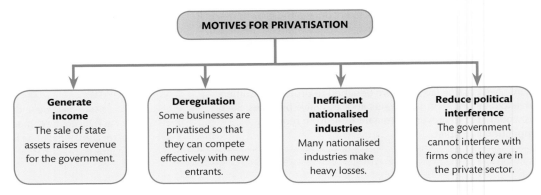

Figure 29.1 *The motives for privatisation.*

In many Eastern European countries there have been huge privatisation programmes. Before the break up of the Soviet Union nearly all production was undertaken in the public sector.

Effects of privatisation

Consumers

- The prices of some services, such as telephone charges have fallen in the United Kingdom.
- Prices of other services such as rail travel, water and gas have risen sharply.
- Some new products and services have arrived due to more innovation.

Workers

- Some newly privatised businesses have laid off workers.
- Some workers have been forced to adopt more flexible working practices.

Firms

- Objectives change. Newly privatised firms aim to make a profit.

- Many firms increase investment following privatisation.

- Merger and takeover activity have often involved newly privatised firms.

Government

- Governments receive the privatisation sale proceeds and the burden of loss-making from nationalised industries has been removed.

- Privatisation may be expensive because lots of money is spent advertising the sale of state assets.

- The government is no longer responsible for managing state-run businesses so it can concentrate on the task of government.

The economy

- If privatisation results in more competition the economy will grow. Costs are lower, waste is reduced and there is more innovation.

- The drive for efficiency may result in job losses and higher benefit payments.

- In some cases public monopolies have become private monopolies. Because of this, consumers may be exploited.

Worked Example

Discuss whether the costs of privatisation outweigh the benefits to the economy. **(6)**

© Edexcel Question paper, January 2012

Newly privatised firms aim to make a profit. Therefore they must operate efficiently and improve productivity to minimise costs. This should help to lower prices. When exposed to competition, newly privatised firms may also be better prepared to take on international rivals. This will help the economy to grow and will generate more employment. In contrast, newly privatised firms might be taken over by overseas operators. As a result, profits will flow abroad. There is also the danger that public sector monopolies might become private sector monopolies. This could result in consumer

exploitation and a reduced incentive to innovate. To conclude, if newly privatised firms become more efficient following privatisation, and if this leads to economic growth and higher levels of employment, the benefits should outweigh the costs for the economy. However, where competition is limited the government should be prepared to monitor firms' activities to protect consumers' interests.

TOP TIP

Some answers to this question were lists of points. Candidates cannot achieve more than half of the marks for just a list of points. There must be some development.

Revision Questions

In 2012, the New South Wales government privatised Sydney Ferries. The state-run ferry company was sold to Harbour City Ferries, a private operator. Their Chief Executive said: 'Our goal is to raise the customer experience to another level gradually by listening to customers and tailor-making improvements around their expectations'. However, opponents of the privatisation suggested that fares would rise and services would be cut.

1 What is meant by the term *privatisation*? **(2)**

2 State **two** possible motives for the privatisation of Sydney Ferries. **(2)**

3 Explain **one** possible effect of the privatisation of Sydney Ferries on (i) customers; (ii) workers. **(4)**

PART 1 Macroeconomic objectives

Chapter 30: Macroeconomic objectives

What is macroeconomics?

Macroeconomics involves looking at the economy as a whole. For example it involves analysing patterns of total income, or spending, total employment, the general price level and trade with other countries.

What are macroeconomic objectives?

When managing the economy the government has aims. These aims, which are summarised in Figure 30.1, are called **macroeconomic objectives**.

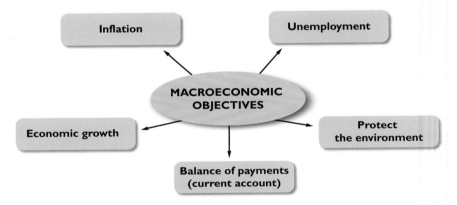

Figure 30.1 *Macroeconomic objectives.*

Economic growth

- Economic growth exists if output grows. It can be measured using **gross domestic product (GDP)**.

- Economic growth raises living standards. People will have more income, improved housing, more leisure time and better public services.

GDP measures the total value of all goods and services produced in an economy over a period of time.

Inflation

- Inflation is a rise in the general price level.

- Governments must reduce inflation because it is harmful. For example if prices rise faster than incomes, living standards will fall because people cannot buy as much.

- Inflation causes uncertainty in the economy because it complicates business decision-making.

- Many governments set targets for inflation. The United Kingdom aims to keep inflation at around 2 per cent per annum.

Unemployment

- People who want a job but cannot find work are said to be unemployed.

- Unemployment is a waste of resources. If people are not working, they do not contribute to output and GDP will be lower.

- Unemployed people face hardship. Their living standards are low compared to those who are in work. If there is no benefit system, the unemployed people may live in poverty. Therefore, governments must reduce unemployment.

The current account

- Most countries trade with others. The goods and services sold overseas are called **exports** and those bought from overseas are called **imports**.

- The **balance of payments** shows the value of all international transactions. The **current account** records the value of goods and services traded.

- Governments may try to balance the current account.

Protecting the environment

- Concerns are being raised about environmental damage. For example there are concerns that global warming could have catastrophic affects on the environment, such as climate change.

- Governments use measures to reduce environmental damage.

Worked Example

China has enjoyed growth rates of around 9 per cent in recent years. The Chinese economy is now the third largest in the world. It produces a lot of manufactured goods which are sold to Western countries.

Complete the sentences below from the following list.

GDP – inflation – unemployment – exports – money

1 (a) China .... manufactured goods to the West. **(1)**

  (b) ....is used to measure economic growth. **(1)**

| (a) | exports |
| (b) | GDP |

TOP TIP ✓

You should find out the rates of growth, inflation and unemployment in the country where you live.

Revision Questions

1 State **two** macroeconomic objectives. **(2)**

2 What does Figure 30.2 show about the performances of the Greek and Indonesian economy? **(4)**

3 Economic growth is the most important macroeconomic objective for a government. Do you agree with this statement? Give reasons for your answer. **(6)**

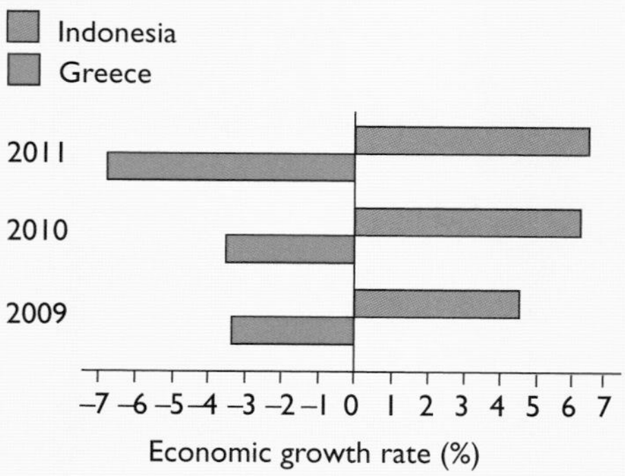

Figure 30.2 *Economic growth in Greece and Indonesia (2009–2011).*

Chapter 31: **Economic growth**

What is economic growth?

- Economic growth exists if **national income** is rising. The most common measure of national income is gross domestic product (GDP).
- In developed countries, growth has averaged 2.5 per cent for many decades. However, recently growth has been negative in some countries.

Total growth and the rate of growth

- Figure 31.1 shows that *total growth* over 5 years is £176bn (17.6 per cent).
- The total growth of 17.6 per cent is greater than the total of 16.5 per cent when the *annual growth rates* are added (3.0 + 3.4 + 3.6 + 4.1 + 2.4).

	Year 0	Year 1	Year 2	Year 3	Year 4	Year 5
Growth rate (GDP)	N/A	3.0%	3.4%	3.6%	4.1%	2.4%
GDP	£1000bn	£1030bn	£1065bn	£1103bn	£1148bn	£1176bn

Figure 31.1 *Growth of an economy.*

The limitations of GDP as a measure of economic growth

- **Inflation** Price increases can distort growth rates. For example if growth is 2.6 per cent and inflation is 2.6 per cent, the economy has not grown.
- **Population changes** If the population increases faster than growth there will be no real increase in growth. The extra income is shared between more people.
- **Statistical errors** Gathering the data to calculate national income is a huge task and errors are common.
- **The hidden economy** Some paid work is unrecorded. For example a friend may drive a family to an airport for £25 cash. This £25 will not be recorded.

The economic cycle

Over time, the rate of growth is likely to fluctuate and GDP may even fall. These fluctuations, shown in Figure 31.2, are referred to as the **economic cycle**.

- **Boom** This is the peak of the cycle. During a boom GDP is growing fast. Demand, job creation, wages, profits and prices may all be rising.
- **Downturn** After a boom, the economy grows at a slower rate. Demand flattens and wage and price increases are slower.
- **Recession or depression** At the bottom of the cycle, GDP may be flat or falling. Economic growth may be negative. Demand falls, unemployment rises and business confidence is low.
- **Recovery** This is when GDP starts to rise again. Businesses and consumers regain their confidence. Demand rises and unemployment falls.

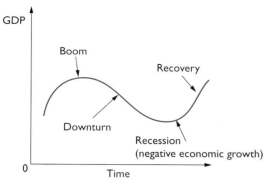

Figure 31.2 *The economic cycle.*

In recent years many European countries have been in recession. They have been stuck at the bottom of the cycle.

The benefits of economic growth

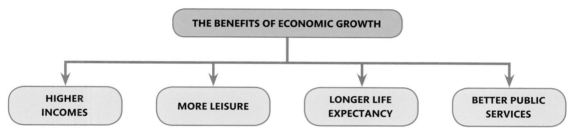

Figure 31.3 *The benefits of economic growth.*

Worked Example

Figure 31.4 shows the economic growth in Ireland in 2007 and 2008

1 *(a)* With reference to the data in Figure 31.4, explain why the economy of Ireland could be described as being in recession. **(3)**

(b) Identify **two** reasons why governments attempt to increase economic growth. **(2)**

© *Edexcel Question paper, June 2011*

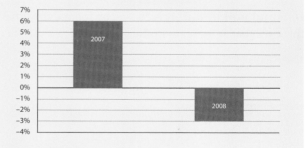

Figure 31.4

1 *(a)* An economy is said to be in recession if output is falling. Figure 31.4 shows that in 2008, economic growth in Ireland was –3 per cent. Therefore, Ireland is in recession.

(b) Higher incomes and provide better public services.

TOP TIP

Remember that economic growth can be negative as it has been in many Western economies since 2008.

Revision Questions

1 Define *economic growth*. **(2)**

2 State **two** limitations of using GDP to measure economic growth. **(2)**

3 Explain what happens when there is a downturn in the economy. **(4)**

Chapter 32: **Inflation**

What is inflation?

Inflation is a rise in the general price level. For example the prices of the goods and services shown in Figure 32.1 have all increased between 2011 and 2012. This is inflation. **Deflation** is the term used to describe a fall in the general price level.

	2011	2012	Increase
Single rail fare—Liverpool to Birmingham	£8	£9	12.5 per cent
Petrol per litre	£131.7	£144.7	9.9 per cent
Chocolate cake	£1.25	£1.50	20 per cent
Aston Villa Season Ticket (cheapest)	£250	£295	18 per cent

Figure 32.1 *Examples of rising prices in the United Kingdom.*

How is inflation measured?

- **Consumer Price Index (CPI)** The prices of about 600 goods and services purchased by several thousand families are recorded each month. An average price change is calculated and then converted into an index number.

- **Retail Price Index (RPI)** This is similar to the CPI but also includes house prices and Council Tax.

What causes inflation?

Demand pull inflation is caused by too much demand in the economy. If **aggregate demand** increases, there will be an increase in the general price level. It could be caused by rising:

- consumer spending

- government spending

- investment by firms

- demand for exports.

> Aggregate demand is total demand in the economy. It includes consumption, investment, government expenditure and exports (imports have to be subtracted, because this is demand for foreign goods).

Cost push inflation

Cost push inflation is caused by rising costs. When costs rise, businesses raise their prices to protect their profit margins. As a result, inflation occurs. For example costs might rise because:

- the cost of imports such as oil rise

- wages rise

- sales taxes such as VAT increase

- businesses increase profit margins.

Money supply inflation

- Some economists say that inflation has only one cause. If the money supply grows too quickly, the general price level will rise.

- Money supply inflation is caused when households, firms or the government borrow more money to fund extra spending. The extra money lent by banks creates more demand and prices rise.

> The money supply is the stock of notes and coins, bank deposits and other financial assets in the economy.

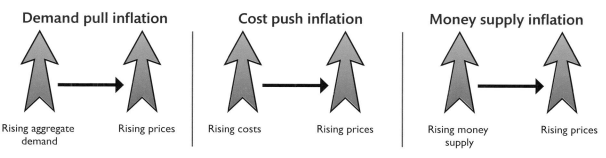

Demand pull inflation	Cost push inflation	Money supply inflation

Rising aggregate demand → Rising prices | Rising costs → Rising prices | Rising money supply → Rising prices

Figure 32.2 *Possible causes of inflation.*

Worked Example

What is meant by cost push inflation? **(3)**

When costs rise businesses put up their prices to protect their profit margins. The result is cost push inflation. Business costs might rise because workers want higher wages or because the government increases VAT. If businesses didn't raise their prices when costs rise, their profits would fall.

TOP TIP ✔

Do not confuse the terms prices and costs. Costs are the expenses firms incur in production. Prices are the amounts paid by customers for goods and services.

Revision Questions

Inflation in Venezuela was 27.6 per cent in 2011. Venezuela had the second-highest inflation rate in the world; only Ethiopia's was higher at 31.5 per cent. It was suggested that inflation in Venezuela was influenced by an expanding money supply and heavy government spending.

1 What is meant by inflation? **(2)**

2 Which of the following is used to measure inflation?
  A Gross Domestic Product (GDP)
  B Consumer Price Index (CPI)
  C Gross National Product (GNP)
  D Changes in share prices **(1)**

3 Explain the difference between demand pull inflation and money supply inflation. **(4)**

Chapter 33: **Consequences of inflation**

Consequences of inflation

Reduced purchasing power

- This means that people cannot buy as much with their income. For example in 1970 in the United Kingdom, the price of a loaf of bread was 9p. In 2012, the same loaf cost £1.

- Living standards fall because people cannot buy as many goods and services.

Reduces the value of savings

- Inflation reduces the value of savings over time. For example if inflation is 7 per cent and the interest rate is 4 per cent, the value of savings has fallen by 3 per cent (7 − 4).

Increased business costs

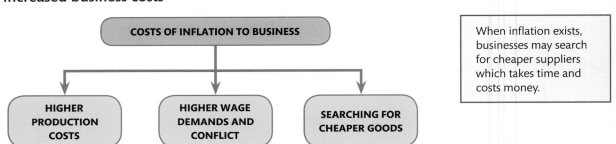

When inflation exists, businesses may search for cheaper suppliers which takes time and costs money.

Figure 33.1 *The costs of inflation to business.*

Balance of payments problems

- If inflation is higher than in other countries, selling in overseas markets is more difficult because export prices are higher.

- If the demand for exports falls, the current account (international trade in goods and services) will be adversely affected.

Unemployment

- Inflation creates uncertainty and firms find it very difficult to plan ahead. They have difficulty in predicting future costs, prices and profits.

- This uncertainty discourages them from investing and job creation is reduced. In some cases, firms actually lay off workers causing unemployment.

Increases in government spending

- Inflation results in higher government spending because much of it is linked to the rate of inflation.

- For example state benefits and pensions are index-linked, which means that they rise automatically each year by the CPI or the Retail Price Index (RPI).

- The wages of public sector workers such as teachers and police officers are also index-linked.

Inflation and the functions of money

The functions of money are summarised in Figure 33.2.

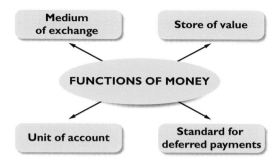

Figure 33.2 *The functions of money.*

High inflation can affect the functions of money.

- If it leads to **hyperinflation** (out-of-control inflation) money may cease to be a medium of exchange. People may find other ways of trading.

- Money is a poor store of value during inflation. The value of savings falls if inflation is higher than interest rates.

- Money may not function as a unit of account because monetary values may become distorted and there is uncertainty about the values of goods.

- Inflation can benefit those who are in debt because, eventually, the amount repaid has less purchasing power than the amount borrowed.

Worked Example

1 *(a)* Identify **one** function of money. *(1)*

   (b) Briefly explain **one** effect of inflation on the function of money you have identified in (a). *(2)*

© Edexcel Question paper, January 2012

1 *(a)* Medium of exchange.

   (b) If inflation is out of control, people may not use money as a medium of exchange. If money loses its value, due to inflation, consumers and traders may use something else as a medium of exchange, such as gold for example.

TOP TIP ✓

Do not confuse the functions of money with the characteristics of money. The functions are the roles money performs in the working of the economy.

Revision Questions

1 Inflation can harm businesses because:

   A import prices fall

   B unemployment falls

   C production costs rise

   D interest rates fall. *(1)*

2 Explain why inflation might result in conflict between workers and employers. *(4)*

3 To what extent might inflation be a problem for a government? *(6)*

Chapter 34: **Unemployment**

How is unemployment measured?

- A person is unemployed if they are seeking work but cannot find a job.

- An International Labour Organisation (ILO) survey may be used to measure unemployment. It involves asking people whether they are in work or not.

- Those who are out of work but do not meet the criteria of unemployment are said to be economically inactive.

- In some countries, the unemployment claimant count is used to measure unemployment. This counts people who claim the unemployment benefit.

Types of unemployment

Cyclical unemployment

- Cyclical unemployment is linked to the economic cycle.

- During a downturn, business activity slows and workers are laid off. This worsens if the economy enters a recession.

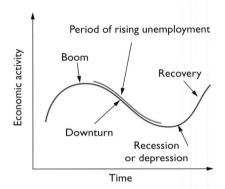

Figure 34.1 *The economic cycle and unemployment.*

Structural unemployment

- Over time, the structure of an economy changes. For example in developed countries, the manufacturing sector declines and the service sector grows.

- A problem with structural unemployment is that workers are slow to switch from one job or region to another. Structural unemployment may persist if labour mobility is poor.

- Figure 34.2 shows three types of structural unemployment.

> Labour mobility is the ability of workers to move from one job to another.

Type	Description
Sectoral	Occurs when a particular industry declines—for example mining in the United Kingdom
Technological	Occurs when machinery is used instead of labour
Regional	Occurs when a geographical area declines—this is more likely to be in an area dominated by one particular industry

Figure 34.2 *Types of structural unemployment.*

Frictional unemployment

- This is short-term unemployment and occurs when people move between jobs. Frictional unemployment always exists and is not a serious problem.

- Unemployment for periods of up to eight weeks is considered to be frictional.

Seasonal unemployment

- This is unemployment at particular times of the year. For example in holiday resorts, the hotels, restaurants and tourist attractions take on more staff during the holiday season and then lay them off during the winter.

Voluntary unemployment

- A minority of people in society choose not to work. These people are said to be voluntarily unemployed.

- People voluntarily unemployed may think that wages are too low or they may not like the idea of work.

Worked Example

Due to the recession, the rate of unemployment in Belgium increased from 2008 to 2009. What is the name given to this type of unemployment?

    A Frictional

    B Seasonal

    C Cyclical   *(1)*

© Edexcel Question paper, May 2012

> **C** is the correct answer. Cyclical unemployment is when people lose their jobs due to a downturn or a recession in the economy. Hopefully people will be re-employed when the economy recovers.

TOP TIP
Make an effort to learn the different types of unemployment. It is easy to mix up some of them.

Revision Questions

The newspaper industry has been in decline since 2000, as web-based advertising has taken over its source of revenue. Employees, such as journalists, printers and distributors, who were dependent upon that industry, have been laid off.

1 Use this case as an example to explain what is meant by *structural unemployment?*   *(3)*

2 Explain the link between labour mobility and structural unemployment.   *(3)*

3 Explain the difference between frictional and seasonal unemployment.   *(4)*

Chapter 35: **Balance of payments on the current account**

Visible and invisible trade

- Goods and services sold overseas are called **exports**.

- Goods and services bought from other countries are called **imports**.

- **Visible trade** involves trade in physical goods (such as clothes, furniture, toys, bicycles and musical instruments) with overseas nations. **The visible balance is sometimes called the balance of trade**.

- **Invisible trade** involves trade in services such as shipping, tourism, financial services and consultancy.

The balance of payments

The balance of payments is a record of all international business transactions.

- The **current account** shows the value of all imports and exports over a period of time. It includes both visible and invisible trade and income or payments resulting from interest, profits and dividends.

- A current account **deficit** means that imports are greater than exports.

- A current account **surplus** means that exports are greater than imports.

> The balance of payments also includes the **capital account**. This records flows of money between countries that result from transactions relating to savings, investments and speculation.

Effects of a current account surplus or deficit

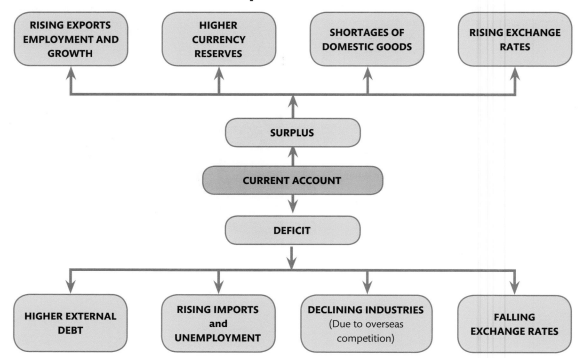

Figure 35.1 *The possible effects of current account surpluses and deficits.*

The balance of payments and the government

- Governments may aim for balance of payments equilibrium.

- This means that over a period of time the value of exports is roughly equal to the value of imports.

- If a balance of payments deficit persists for too long the economy would suffer.

Worked Example

Figure 35.1 shows the balance of payments on current account for Vietnam from 2007 to 2009

1 **(a)** Using the data in Figure 35.2, describe what happened to the balance of payments on current account from 2007 to 2008. **(2)**

The balance of payments on a country's current account shows the trade in visible and invisible imports and exports.

(b) Give an example of a *visible import*. **(1)**

(c) Give an example of an *invisible import*. **(1)**

© Edexcel Question paper, January 2012

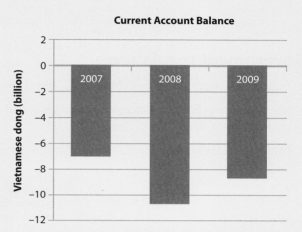

Figure 35.2 *Vietnam current account balance 2007–2009.*

> 1 **(a)** In 2007 Vietnam had a balance of payments deficit on the current account. This means that imports were greater than exports. In 2008 this deficit worsened. It rose from 7bn dongs to about 10.5 bn dongs.
>
> **(b)** Cars.
>
> **(c)** Tourism.

TOP TIP ✓

It is important to use the term 'deficit' when answering (a). In (b) and (c) no marks were awarded for using synonyms, that is visible = goods or invisible = services.

Revision Questions

1 Which of the following is an example of an invisible export?

    A The purchase of foreign exchange

    B The sale of aircraft components overseas

    C The purchase of oil from overseas

    D Foreign tourists spending money in domestic restaurants **(1)**

2 Explain **two** effects of a balance of payments surplus. **(4)**

3 To what extent is a balance of payments deficit a problem for a government? **(6)**

Chapter 36: **Protection of the environment**

Environmental protection

Governments are becoming increasingly concerned about the environment. As a result many governments are:

- tackling the effects of climate change by cutting greenhouse gas emissions
- encouraging activities that minimise carbon emissions, waste and the use of non-renewable resources.

Government regulation

- Legislation, regulations, guidelines and codes of practice exist to help protect the environment.
- Some countries have an **Environment Agency** which takes action against those who break environmental laws.
- Examples of legislation are outlined briefly in Figure 36.1

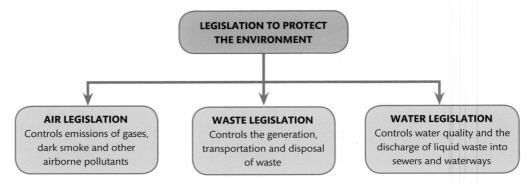

Figure 36.1 *Examples of environmental legislation.*

Taxation

- Many governments impose taxes on those that damage the environment.
- Taxation ensures that the social costs resulting from production and consumption are met by those who impose them.
- Some governments tax petrol heavily to reduce car use and carbon emissions.

Other methods of protection

- *Subsidies* such as grants and tax allowances can be offered as an incentive to reduce activities that damage the environment. For example a firm might receive a subsidy if it builds a plastics recycling plant.
- *Compensation* may be paid to the victims of environmental damage. For example people living nearby airports may receive money for double glazing and other types of insulation.
- *Recycling* involves collecting waste material such as paper, plastic, glass, aluminium or steel, and producing a new raw material from that waste. This helps to reduce waste and saves non-renewable resources.

- ***International targets*** have been set to reduce global pollution. One example is the **Kyoto Protocol**. This was signed by 183 countries in Kyoto, Japan, and came into force in 2005.

- ***Road pricing and charges*** Charging road users should discourage car use and help to reduce congestion and pollution.

Congestion Charges are used in London, Singapore and Stockholm.

PART 1 Chapter 36: Protection of the environment

Worked Example

1 **(a)** Government policies targeting environmental protection can include:

    A subsidies for car ownership

    B subsidies for environmentally friendly power generation

    C taxes on income

    D taxes on profits   **(1)**

  (b) Explain why you have chosen your answer to (a).   **(2)**

© Edexcel Sample Assessment Material

> **1** **(a)** **B** is the correct answer.
>
>   **(b)** A lot of power generation involves burning fossil fuels such as gas and oil. This is likely to contribute to global warming and climate change. If subsidies are given for environmentally friendly power generation, such as solar power, the burning of fossil fuels should be reduced. As a result, there should be less environmental damage.

TOP TIP

You do not need to learn about specific pieces of environmental legislation when revising this area.

Revision Questions

Chinese lawmakers want better legislation to guarantee drinking water quality. The development of heavy chemical industry along major rivers in China is often to blame for the country's deteriorating water quality. According to government surveys, about 11.4 per cent of water supplies to cities are unsafe.

1 Why do Chinese lawmakers want better environmental legislation?   **(2)**

2 Discuss the view that legislation is a more powerful tool than taxation when protecting the environment.   **(6)**

3 Explain how subsidies might be used to protect the environment.   **(4)**

PART 2 Policies: to deal with economic growth, inflation, unemployment, the balance of payments on current account and protection of the environment

Chapter 37: Economic policy and policy instruments

What are policy instruments?

- **Policy instruments** are the tools used by the government to achieve its macroeconomic objectives.

- They are economic variables such as the rate of interest, rates of taxation and levels of government expenditure. They can be influenced by the government.

> Changes in policy instruments can affect other variables in the economy such as aggregate demand, inflation, unemployment and GDP.

Economic policy

- Policy instruments and other measures are used by the government when implementing its **economic policy**.

- Economic policies are the actions a government might take when controlling the economy and trying to achieve its macroeconomic objectives.

Fiscal policy and monetary policy

Both fiscal policy and monetary policy are used to influence aggregate demand in the economy. They are summarised in Figure 37.1.

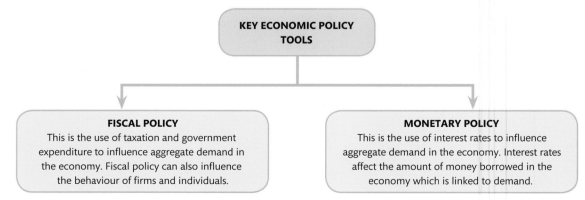

Figure 37.1 *Fiscal policy and monetary policy.*

Supply side policies

Supply side policies aim to increase the productive potential of the economy. They promote economic growth by increasing aggregate supply. Supply side policies often focus on three specific markets.

- **Labour market** Supply side policies have tried to make labour markets more flexible by weakening trade unions and improving the quality of labour through, for example, training and education.

- **Capital market** In some countries, measures have been used to increase investment by firms. For example the tax system has been used to increase the money available to firms for investment.

- **Goods market** The aim here has often been to promote more competition in goods markets, for example through privatisation and deregulation.

Other economic policies

- **Environmental policies** such as taxation and regulation are used to help protect the environment.

- **Exchange rate policies** are used to influence the current account on the balance of payments. These involve influencing the rate at which one country's currency exchanges against that of another.

Worked Example

A government's use of taxation and government expenditure to achieve economic objectives is called

    A   Fiscal policy

    B   Monetary policy

    C   Supply side policy   *(1)*

© Edexcel Question paper, May 2012

> **A** is the correct answer. Fiscal policy involves using taxation and government expenditure to influence the level of aggregate demand in the economy.

TOP TIP

Fiscal policy, monetary policy and supply side policy are discussed in more detail in Chapters 38, 39 and 40.

Revision Questions

In recent years many Western economies have been in recession. In an effort to reduce their debt, governments have cut their expenditure greatly. There have also been numerous tax increases.

Complete the sentences below from the following list.

aggregate demand – privatisation

fiscal policy – supply side policy

monetary policy – interest rates

1. *(a)* Cutting government expenditure is an example of .... *(1)*

    (b) Raising taxes will reduce ....in the economy. *(1)*

    (c) Lowering ....can stimulate demand in economies. *(1)*

2. Explain how interest rates are linked to aggregate demand. *(4)*

3. Explain the aim of supply side policies. *(4)*

Chapter 38: **Fiscal policy**

Fiscal policy and the budget

- Fiscal policy is to do with government spending, taxation and borrowing.

- Each year governments prepare a **budget**. This shows how much is going to be spent in each category of expenditure and how the money will be raised.

> If a government spends more than it receives, there will be a **budget deficit**. This means that the government must borrow money to fund the deficit. If expenditure exceeds tax revenues, there will be a **budget surplus**.

Government expenditure

- The amount spent by governments varies between different countries.

- The main items of government expenditure include social protection such as job seekers allowance, pensions and disability allowances, healthcare, education, defence, debt interest, social services and transport.

Taxation

Governments impose taxes to:

- pay for public sector services

- discourage certain activities like smoking or alcohol consumption

- control aggregate demand in the economy

- reduce the gap between the rich and the poor.

Direct and indirect taxes

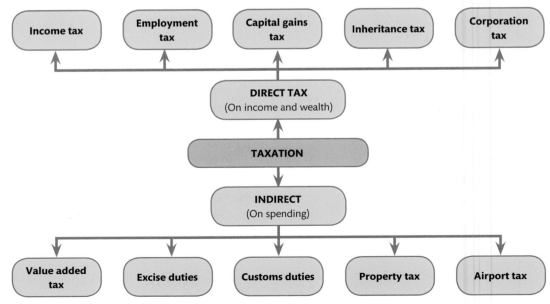

Figure 38.1 *Examples of direct and indirect taxes used in many countries.*

Environmental taxes

- **Landfill tax** is imposed on the disposal of waste in landfill sites.
- **Climate change levy** is levied on the power industry to reduce emissions.
- **Aggregates levy** is a tax on quarrying to reduce environmental damage.

Managing the economy

- Fiscal policy is used to influence aggregate demand in the economy.

- **Expansionary fiscal policy** is used to stimulate demand and involves increasing the budget deficit by spending more or taxing less.

- **Contractionary fiscal policy** is used to cut demand and involves reducing the budget deficit by spending less or raising taxes.

Objective	Fiscal policy	Explanation
Inflation	Contractionary	Dampen demand by cutting expenditure or raising taxes. This will reduce the pressure on prices.
Unemployment	Expansionary	Firms will produce more and take on more workers if demand from consumers and the government increases.
Economic growth	Expansionary	Government spending such as investment in the infrastructure will help stimulate growth. Tax cuts may be less effective because some money is spent on imports.
Current account deficit	Contractionary	If aggregate demand is dampened this will reduce the demand for imports.

Figure 38.2 *The use of fiscal policy to achieve macroeconomic objectives.*

Worked Example

1 *(a)* Use examples to distinguish between direct and indirect taxation. *(4)*

(b) Identify **two** main items of government expenditure. *(2)*

© Edexcel Question paper, May 2012

1 *(a)* Direct taxation is a tax on individuals or firms. Direct taxes usually target income and wealth. Most countries have an income tax on the income earned by individuals. There may also be taxes on company profits, such as corporation tax. Indirect taxes are imposed on spending. Common examples include value added tax which is a type of sales tax.

(b) Education and defence.

TOP TIP

In (b) only the **main** items of government expenditure such as education, healthcare, social security, pensions, defence and law and order were awarded marks.

Revision Questions

1 State **two** aims of taxation. *(2)*

2 Explain how the government can reduce inflation using fiscal policy. *(4)*

3 To reduce unemployment in the economy, the government should reduce taxation rather than increase government spending. Do you agree with this statement? Give reasons for your answer. *(6)*

Chapter 39: **Monetary policy**

What is monetary policy?

Monetary policy involves controlling aggregate demand by adjusting **interest rates** or the **money supply**.

Interest rates

- Interest is the price paid to lenders for borrowed money.

- A lot of demand is fuelled by borrowed money so the level of interest rates can have an important effect in the economy.

- In many countries interest rates are set by the central bank. All other interest rates in the economy are influenced by this **base rate**.

How does the rate of interest affect the decisions of consumers and firms?

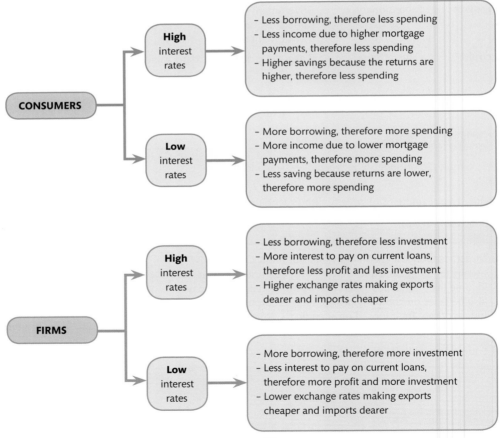

Figure 39.1 *The impact of high and low interest rates on consumers and firms.*

Money supply

- Aggregate demand in the economy is influenced by the **money supply**. This is the total amount of money that circulates in the economy.

- Defining the money supply is not easy. However, basically, it is all the notes and coins in the economy plus any money held in bank accounts.

> Trying to control the growth of the money supply is not easy because it is difficult to define the money supply.

Monetary policy and the macroeconomic objectives

Objective	Monetary policy	Explanation
Reduce inflation	Tight monetary policy	Higher interest rates and a lower money supply will dampen aggregate demand in the economy. This should reduce pressure on prices.
Reduce unemployment	Loose monetary policy	Lower interest rates and a growing money supply will help increase demand. Firms will respond by taking on more workers and producing more output.
Promote economic growth	Loose monetary policy	Lower interest rates and a growing money supply will encourage more investment and increase demand. This might also help the economy to move out of a recession.
Cut a current account deficit	Lower interest rates	Lower interest rates will lower the exchange rate which makes exports cheaper and imports dearer. So demand for exports should rise and the demand for imports fall.

Figure 39.2 *Monetary policy and macroeconomic objectives.*

Worked Example

Briefly explain **two** reasons why an increase in the rate of interest might lead to an increase in the level of unemployment. **(4)**

© *Edexcel Question paper, January 2012*

> Higher interest rates raise the cost of borrowing. This discourages the purchase of goods like consumer durables which are often funded from borrowed money. A fall in demand for such goods will mean that firms have to cut production and lay off workers.
>
> It could also be argued that people save more when interest rates are higher. This means they will spend less, and therefore demand in the economy falls. Again, firms will respond by cutting production and making workers redundant.

TOP TIP ✓

It is also possible to discuss how firms would react to lower interest rates. However, some candidates argued that firms would not take out loans to expand when interest rates rise. This would not necessarily lead to unemployment. It means that further **employment** would not be created.

Revision Questions

1 An increase in the rate of interest is an instrument of

    A Fiscal policy

    B Monetary policy

    C Supply side policy

    D Regional policy   *(1)*

2 What is meant by the money supply? **(2)**

3 The use of monetary policy is the best way to reduce inflation. Do you agree with this statement? Give reasons for your answer. **(6)**

Chapter 40: **Supply side policies**

What are supply side policies?

Supply side polices are used to increase aggregate supply in the economy. They help the economy to grow and can lower unemployment and inflation. Supply side policies operate over a longer term than demand side policies and aim to:

- improve labour flexibility
- promote competition through privatisation, deregulation and helping small firms
- increase both public and private sector investment.

Labour market

Aggregate supply will increase if labour productivity is higher.

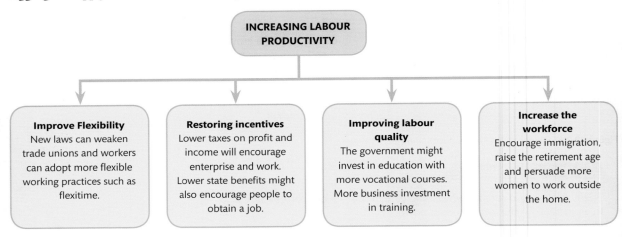

Figure 40.1 *Examples of supply side policies to increase labour productivity.*

Product markets

Some supply side policies help to improve efficiency in product markets. They aim to promote competition and reduce 'red tape' in business. For example:

- **Privatisation** Privatisation breaks up state monopolies and promotes competition which should improve efficiency, raise quality and lower prices.
- **Deregulation** Many governments have removed rules and regulations that are said to discourage business activity and prevent competition.
- **Helping small firms** Aggregate supply will increase if more small firms are started. Governments have helped small firms by lowering taxes on small firms, setting up advisory centres and reducing 'red tape'.

> Examples of deregulation in the United Kingdom include the deregulation of the stock market allowing more firms to trade in shares, relaxing restrictions on trading hours and allowing competition in the provision of postal services.

Capital markets

Aggregate supply will increase if there is more investment in the economy.

- In the public sector, the government can help by investing more in the infrastructure, such as education, training and healthcare.

- Private sector investment can be encouraged if the economy is stable, interest rates are low and if financial incentives exist for potential investors.

Worked Example

To what extent are supply side policies likely to be successful in reducing unemployment? *(6)*

© *Edexcel Question paper, January 2012*

Supply side policies may help to reduce unemployment. For example, if the government invests more in education and training, the quality of labour would improve. This means that people would be more employable. Therefore, if firms take on more workers unemployment will fall. Also, if more businesses set up as a result of privatisation and deregulation, more jobs will be created and unemployment will fall. However, it is important to note that supply side policies operate over a longer period of time than demand side policies. Also, some types of unemployment, like cyclical unemployment, may not be resolved by supply side policies. A reduction in cyclical unemployment may require a demand stimulus. The extent to which supply side policies reduce unemployment depends on the state of the economy and the types of unemployment it faces.

TOP TIP

It is important to recognise that supply side measures operate over a longer time period than demand side policies.

Revision Questions

Growth in India has fallen from around 9 per cent in 2008 to 7 per cent in 2011. At the same time, inflation has increased. Some have argued that supply side policies are needed to restore higher growth rates and to help reduce inflation. Supply side policies are already being used in India. For example the government is investing a great deal in road-building to improve transport communications. However, a lot more is needed, for example tax cuts, less regulation and investment in energy generation.

1 Which of the following is a supply side measure?

    A Lower interest rates

    B Higher interest rates

    C Government investment in education

    D Cuts in government expenditure   *(1)*

2 How will investment in road-building increase aggregate supply in India?   *(4)*

3 Explain two supply side policies that might help to reduce inflation in India.   *(4)*

PART 3 Relationship between objectives and policies

Chapter 41: Relationship between objectives and policies

The effects of policy measures on macroeconomic objectives

Policies aim to promote economic growth, reduce unemployment and inflation, balance the current account and protect the environment.

> The policies used will depend on the economic circumstances at the time, and can be both positive and negative.

The possible effects of expansionary fiscal policy

Positive	Explanation
Lower unemployment	As aggregate demand rises, firms will respond by taking on more workers to produce more. Higher government spending may create jobs directly—for example more teachers.
More growth	With more spending and public sector investment there will be an increase in GDP.
Better public services	More government spending should mean better public services—for example smaller class sizes and shorter waiting lists for hospital treatment.
More tax revenue	Some economists argue that tax revenues rise when tax rates are lower. There is less tax avoidance and more profit and income to tax.
Negative	**Explanation**
Higher inflation	The increase in aggregate demand might cause demand pull inflation, especially if the economy has limited capacity.
More imports	The extra income from tax cuts may increase the demand for imports. This could worsen the current account.
More debt	If government spending is higher and taxes are lower, the government will have to borrow more which will increase debt.

Figure 41.1 *The effects of expansionary fiscal policy.*

The possible effects of contractionary fiscal policy

Positive	Explanation
Lower inflation	Aggregate demand will be dampened and this will reduce pressure on prices.
Less debt	Government finances will improve with less spending and more tax revenues.
Less imports	Consumers will spend less on imports because they have less disposable income.
Negative	**Explanation**
Higher unemployment	As aggregate demand falls, firms will lay off workers because they do not need to produce as much. Lower government spending may result in fewer jobs—for example nurses and police officers.
Poorer public services	Less government spending may lead to a reduction in services—for example fewer university places or less frequent refuse collection.
Less growth	With less spending and cuts in investment, GDP growth may slow or even fall.

Figure 41.2 *The effects of contractionary fiscal policy.*

The possible effects of tight monetary policy

Positive effects Higher interest rates will:

- discourage borrowing, reduce demand and lower inflation
- encourage saving and benefit those, like pensioners, who rely on savings
- strengthen the exchange rate making imports cheaper.

Negative effects Higher interest rates will

- discourage borrowing, reduce economic growth and increase unemployment
- increase mortgage payments, reduce demand and result in unemployment
- raise business costs, reduce profits and reduce investment
- strengthen exchange rates and increase the price of exports.

The possible effects of loose monetary policy

Positive effects Lower interest rates will:

- encourage borrowing, increase aggregate demand, create jobs and growth
- cut the exchange rate, lower export prices and improve the current account
- lower the cost of servicing government debt which is good for taxpayers
- encourage firms to invest which may improve efficiency.

Negative effects Lower interest rates will:

- increase demand and cause inflation if aggregate supply is inadequate
- increase demand and increase imports which will worsen the current account
- reduce the exchange rate, raise the price of imports and result in inflation.

Trade-offs between objectives

- Governments may have to accept trade-offs between macroeconomic objectives.

- For example contractionary fiscal policy may reduce inflation but also increase unemployment.

Worked Example

One policy to reduce the rate of inflation is raising the rate of interest. Assess the effects of this policy on other objectives. *(6)*

© *Edexcel Sample Assessment Material*

> Higher interest rates will discourage borrowing, encourage saving, dampen aggregate demand and relieve inflationary pressures in the economy. However, this may have a negative impact on other macroeconomic objectives. It may reduce economic growth and raise unemployment. With less demand in the economy firms will not have to produce as much output, and therefore will lay off workers. This will also slow down growth in national income because less is being produced. However, these effects depend on the state of the economy. If the economy is at, or close to, full employment with no spare capacity, the adverse effects of higher interest rates may not be so severe. The impact on unemployment and growth may be tolerable.

TOP TIP
Remember that questions with 6 marks require some evaluation.

Revision Questions

1 State **two** positive effects of loose monetary policy. *(2)*

2 Explain how contractionary fiscal policy can have negative economic impacts. *(4)*

3 A government will always face trade-offs when implementing policies to achieve objectives? Do you agree with this statement? Give reasons for your answer. *(6)*

SECTION D: THE GLOBAL ECONOMY

PART 1 Globalisation

Chapter 42: Globalisation and multinational companies

What is globalisation?

Globalisation is the growing interdependence and integration of the world's economies.

- Goods and services are traded freely across international borders. There are no government restrictions which prevent trading.
- To a large extent people are free to live and work in any country they choose.
- There is a high level of interdependence between nations.
- Capital can flow freely between different countries and shares can be bought in foreign companies.

Reasons for globalisation

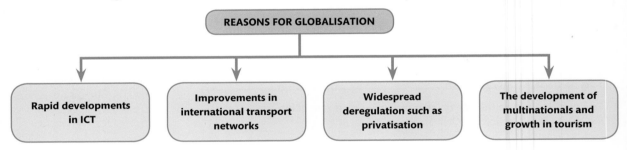

Figure 42.1 *Reasons for globalisation.*

Government and globalisation

Globalisation can only flourish if governments are committed to it. For example

- countries cannot trade if the government keeps international borders closed
- international trade will be very limited if governments use **protectionism**
- people cannot be free to live and work overseas if borders are closed
- firms cannot develop overseas if planning permission is denied.

Multinationals

A multinational company (MNC) is a large and powerful firm that sells goods and services into global markets and owns production plants and other operating facilities all over the world.

The number of MNCs has increased from about 7,000 in the beginning of the 1970s to about 78,000 in 2005. They contribute about 10 per cent to world GDP and about 66 per cent to global exports. MNCs now employ about 73m workers which is about 3 per cent of the global workforce.

Why do multinationals exist?

```
                    ┌──────────────────────────────────┐
                    │  WHY DO MULTINATIONALS EXIST?     │
                    └──────────────────────────────────┘
```

ECONOMIES OF SCALE
MNCs are large and powerful.
They sell to global markets and
produce more than those who
just sell to domestic markets. They
can therefore lower costs.

MARKETING
Some MNCs exist because they
have established a very strong
brand and have sold it all over the
world. They use heavy advertising
and patents to prevent copying.

**TECHNICAL AND FINANCIAL
SUPERIORITY**
MNCs have developed complex
technologies, built up a bank of
knowledge and can afford to invest
heavily in R &D. They also have the
resources to take risks and diversify.

Figure 42.2 *Why do multinationals exist?*

Worked Example

The increasing interdependence and integration of the world's economies is
known as

    A   globalisation

    B   the emerging economies

    C   the World Trade Organization

    D   the developed countries   *(1)*

© *Edexcel Question paper, January 2012*

> **A** is the correct answer. Globalisation is the growing interdependence
> and integration of the world's economies.

TOP TIP
MNCs benefit considerably
from economies of scale. Look
at Chapter 19 to ensure that
you know enough about this
concept.

Revision Questions

India-based Tata is a multinational company. It operates
in seven different business sectors: engineering,
services, ITC, energy, materials, consumer products and
services. It employs 425,000 staff, has a turnover of
about US$84bn and sells to over 80 different countries.

1 State **two** reasons for the development of
    globalisation.   *(2)*

2 Explain what is meant by the growing
    interdependence of the world's economies.   *(4)*

3 Explain how Tata might have technical and financial
    superiority as an MNC.   *(4)*

Chapter 43: **Foreign direct investment and development aid**

What is meant by foreign direct investment?

- **Foreign direct investment (FDI)** occurs when a company makes an investment such as the construction of a factory in a foreign country.
- FDI also includes the purchase of shares in a foreign business.
- Most FDI is undertaken by multinational companies (MNCs).
- A common approach to FDI is for a foreign company to join forces with a company in the host nation to develop a business venture.

Governments and FDI

To encourage FDI governments:

- offer tax breaks, subsidies, grants and low interest loans
- relax regulations to make it easier for foreign firms to invest
- invest in their own infrastructure
- invest in education so that locals can obtain jobs with foreign companies.

Development aid

- This is money and other forms of assistance given to developing countries by governments in developed countries.
- Its purpose is to help the long-term development of a nation.
- It is not to be confused with humanitarian aid which is designed to help resolve short-term problems, such as starvation or the effects of a natural disaster.

> In 2011, the amount of aid given to developing nations was US$133.5 billion. About a quarter of this aid went to sub-Saharan African nations.

Development aid is needed for a range of projects. Examples include:

- clean water projects and healthcare programmes
- education and training programmes
- agricultural projects such as irrigation and land reclamation
- infrastructure development such as roads, generators, bridges and airports
- access to technology such as computers and machinery.

Types of development aid

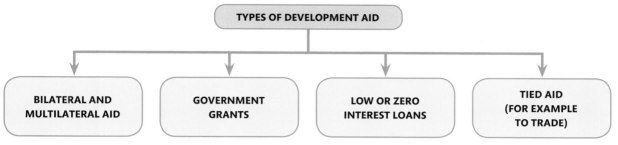

Figure 43.1 *Types of development aid.*

FDI, development aid and globalisation

- Both FDI and development aid will help globalisation to gather pace.

- The money and employment that developing countries receive from FDI and aid will promote economic growth.

- As developing countries become less poor, they provide market opportunities for MNCs.

Revision Questions

1 Identify **two** types of aid that might be given to a developing country. *(2)*

2 Explain how **one** of your answers above might benefit a country. *(4)*

3 To what extent can a government encourage foreign direct investment? *(6)*

Chapter 44: Winners and losers from globalisation

Benefits to developed countries of globalisation

- Higher profits for multinationals (MNCs) which are often repatriated
- Higher income, output and employment for the nation
- Lower prices due to competition
- Increase in the labour supply due to greater freedom of movement
- Greater consumer choice as more firms export their goods
- The threat of military conflict is reduced due to more cooperation.

Benefits to developing nations of globalisation

The effects of globalisation on developing countries are often linked to the activities of MNCs in these countries. Benefits might include:

- increase in GDP and higher living standards
- increase in tax revenue from the location of the MNCs
- increase in exports resulting from the output of newly located MNCs
- increase in employment from MNCs and from local suppliers
- new technologies and modern working practices are introduced
- improved human capital quality due to on-the-job learning given by MNCs
- more enterprise development—for example MNCs often encourage local suppliers
- reduction in Third World debt because developing countries can repay debts more easily and developed nations have more money to donate.

In 2005, the G8 nations agreed to write off the entire US$40 billion debt owed by 18 Highly Indebted Poor Countries to the World Bank, the International Monetary Fund and the African Development Fund.

Disadvantages of globalisation

DISADVANTAGES OF GLOBALISATION

ENVIRONMENTAL DAMAGE
As economies grow, there are more cars and aeroplanes. This increases greenhouse gases which cause global warming. In addition, more non-renewable resources are used.

EXPLOITATION OF DEVELOPING COUNTRIES
MNCs often pay very low wages.
Most of the profit made is sent to the MNC's country.
Tax paid is often low.
Developing nations rely too much on primary industry.
MNCs out-compete local businesses.

HIGHER COMMODITY PRICES
Rapid global growth in the 2000s caused a surge in commodity prices such as rice and wheat. These are often the main food sources for developing nations.

INTERDEPENDENCE
Events in one country can have an impact on others. For example recessions in the Eurozone in 2011–2012 had an impact in China. Growth in China fell from over 9 per cent to around 7 per cent.

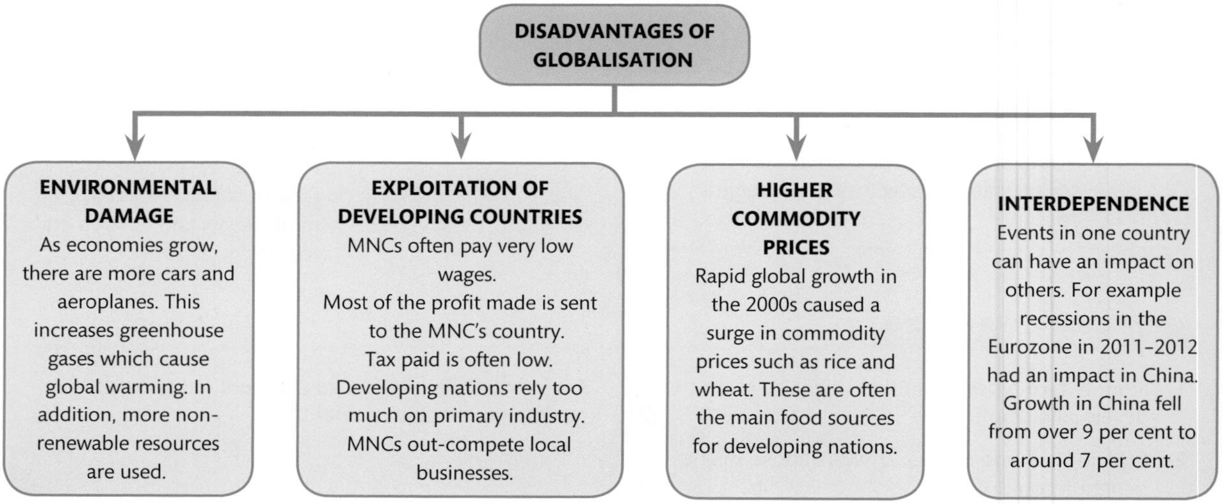

Figure 44.1 *Disadvantages of globalisation.*

Development gap

- Globalisation results in economic growth and development. However, the pace is not likely to be the same in all countries.

- Some argue that developed nations benefit most because they have the resources to exploit the forces of globalisation.

- As a result, the gap between the rich and poor has increased.

Worked Example

Will the setting up of a multinational in a developing country always lead to an improvement in the standard of living for the people of that country? Give reasons for your answer. **(6)**

© Edexcel Question paper, January 2012

> When multinationals set up operations in developing countries they create jobs. Not only will there be direct employment, where locals work for the MNC, but there may be indirect employment. This is where local businesses have to employ more workers to supply the MNCs. This increase in employment will help to raise the local people's living standards. MNCs may pay tax on profits and workers may pay income tax. With the extra revenue the government can provide more public services which will also improve living standards.
>
> However, it is often argued that MNCs exploit developing countries. For example, they may pay low wages and destroy local businesses because they are too competitive. This means that incomes may not improve very much and unemployment rises because local firms collapse. This will reduce living standards.
>
> Overall, the impact on living standards after the arrival of an MNC may depend on the government. If there are controls on wages, and if local businesses are protected, the benefits are likely to outweigh the drawbacks and living standards will improve.

TOP TIP ✓

Although there are examples of MNCs exploiting developing countries, many MNCs are socially responsible and would prefer to avoid the bad publicity associated with exploitation.

Revision Questions

Globalisation has led to an increase in the transportation of raw materials and food. Earlier, people used to consume locally grown food, but now people also consume imported products. The amount of fuel used in transporting these products has increased air pollution. It has also led to more noise pollution and landscape disturbance. Transportation also consumes non-renewable resources such as oil.

1. State **two** benefits of globalisation to developed countries. **(2)**

2. Using examples from the case above, explain **two** drawbacks of globalisation for developed countries. **(4)**

3. Explain how globalisation results in interdependence. **(4)**

Heavy smog in Beijing caused by vehicle emissions

PART 2 International trade
Chapter 45: International trade

International trade

International trade benefits the world. It helps to raise living standards and results in higher levels of output and income. The specific reasons for international trade are shown in Figure 45.1.

Figure 45.1 *Specific reasons for international trade.*

Advantages of free trade

Free trade exists if governments allow open access to its markets. This means there are no restrictions on the amount of goods coming in. The main advantages of free trade include more choice, competition and growth.

More choice

- Goods can be obtained that are impossible to produce due to climatic conditions.

- Raw materials that are not available such as oil, gold and iron ore can be bought.

- Goods and services that other countries produce more cheaply can be imported.

More competition

- Free trade provides competition for domestic producers because most countries import goods that they can also produce themselves.

- Competition will put pressure on domestic producers to lower their costs, produce high-quality goods and be more inventive.

More growth

- International trade extends the advantages from specialisation. If countries specialise in the production of goods in which they are more efficient, the global economy will benefit.

- Goods and services all over the world will be produced in locations where costs are minimised. This means that consumers all over the world can buy goods at the lowest possible prices.

- If countries are free to specialise and trade with one another, firms will be selling to larger markets. This allows them to exploit economies of scale, lower their costs and improve efficiency.

Disadvantages of free trade

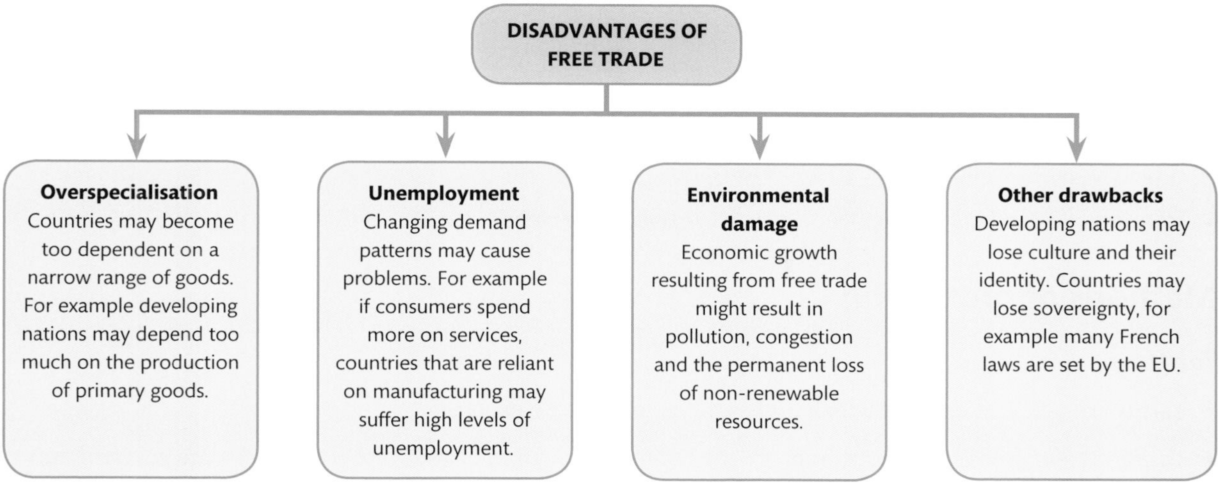

Figure 45.2 *Disadvantages of free trade.*

Worked Example

Briefly explain **two** reasons why free trade may be considered a disadvantage to developing countries. *(4)*

© *Edexcel Question paper, January 2012*

One of the possible disadvantages that developing countries might encounter as a result of free trade is overspecialisation. International trade encourages countries to specialise in the production of those goods which they can produce most efficiently. However, this has often led to developing nations relying too heavily on the production of primary products. Relying on a narrow industrial base can be risky. It is better to develop a range of industries.

Another possible problem is that businesses in developing countries may not be able to compete with firms selling cheap imports. Such firms might be powerful MNCs with years of experience and huge resources. This could lead to a decline in domestic industry resulting in unemployment and falling growth.

TOP TIP ✓

When answering this question a lot of students could not identify the disadvantages of free trade for developing countries. Take time to check that you understand them.

Revision Questions

1 State **two** specific reasons for international trade. *(2)*

2 How might firms lower their average costs as a result of free trade? *(2)*

3 The advantages of international trade outweigh the disadvantages. Do you agree with this statement? Give reasons for your answer. *(6)*

Chapter 46: **Protectionism**

What is protectionism?

- Some governments may believe that restricting trade can be justified.

- A restriction in trade is called **protectionism**.

- Measures designed to restrict trade are called **trade barriers**.

Methods of protection

Tariffs

- Tariffs are taxes on imports which makes these goods more expensive.

- Tariffs cut demand for imports, improve the balance of payments and raise revenue for the government.

- In Figure 46.1A, when the government imposes a tariff, the price rises from P_1 to P_2. As a result, the amount traded in the market falls from Q_1 to Q_2. These changes are caused by a shift to the left in the supply curve from S_1 to S_2.

Quotas

- A quota is a physical limit on the amount of a good allowed into the country.

- If a limit is imposed on the quantity of imports, domestic producers will have a bigger share of the market.

- In Figure 46.1A, the effect in the market of a quota is the same as that of a tariff. The supply curve shifts to the left from S_1 to S_2 forcing a price increase from P_1 to P_2.

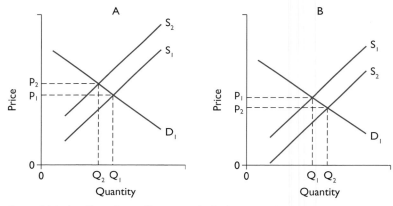

Figure 46.1 *The effect of a tariff, quota and subsidy in a market.*

Subsidies

- This involves giving financial support to exporters or the domestic producers that face competition from imports. Subsidies will lower prices for consumers.

- In Figure 46.1B, before a subsidy is granted the equilibrium price in the market is P_1. The effect of a subsidy is to lower production costs and shift the supply curve to the right from S_1 to S_2. The new equilibrium price is P_2 which is lower than P_1.

Administrative barriers

- Administrative barriers restrict imports by insisting that imported goods meet strict regulations and specifications.

- For example a shipment of toys from a country might be returned if they fail to meet strict health and safety regulations.

Reasons for protectionism

Dumping is where an overseas firm sells huge quantities of a good at below cost in the domestic market. Dumping may be used, for example, to sell off surplus stocks or to put pressure on domestic producers.

Figure 46.2 *Reasons for protectionism.*

Problems of protectionism

Loss of free trade benefits

- Higher prices and less consumer choice
- Lower growth, unemployment and reduced living standards all over the world

Retaliation

- Protectionism may lead to a trade war where one country erects barriers and then those that are affected do exactly the same in retaliation.

Other policies may be more effective

- There may be better ways to protect domestic industries.
- The government could, for example, use supply side policies to help firms.

PART 2 Chapter 46: Protectionism

Worked Example

Briefly explain **one** other way, apart from quotas and tariffs, in which a government can reduce imports. (2)

© Edexcel Question paper, May 2012

> One other way to reduce imports is to impose administrative barriers to trade. These restrict imports by insisting that imported goods meet strict regulations and specifications. For example, a shipment of toys from a country might be returned if they fail to meet strict health and safety regulations.

TOP TIP
Some administrative barriers may not ban imports, but they work because they make it difficult or time-consuming to supply the market.

Revision Questions

1 Which of the following describes a tariff?

   A A physical limit on the quantity imported

   B An administrative restriction

   C A subsidy to domestic producers

   D A tax on imports (1)

2 Draw a diagram to show the effect of a subsidy to an exporter. (4)

3 Are quotas more effective than tariffs in reducing imports? Justify your answer. (5)

Question 3 © Edexcel Question paper, May 2012

Chapter 47: **World trade patterns and trading blocs**

Increase in world trade

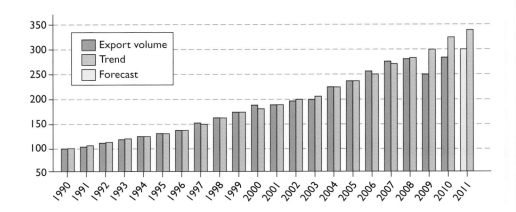

Figure 47.1 *Volume of world merchandise exports 1990–2011.*

Figure 47.1 shows that world trade has grown enormously in the last 20 years. Why?

- Better transport and communications
- Relaxing of trade barriers
- Development of multinationals
- Increased travel and more consumer awareness
- Break up of the Soviet Union
- New trade agreements

What is a trading bloc?

- **Trading blocs** are groups of countries situated in the same region that join together and make a free trade area. Trade between members will be completely free of all trade barriers.
- Trading blocs may have a common tariff on imports from non-member countries.

> The number of trading blocs grew fast in the 1960s and 1970s and again in the 1990s. Examples include: The EU (European Union) which is made up of 27 European countries, NAFTA (North American Free Trade Agreement) whose members are the United States, Canada and Mexico, and CARICOM (The Caribbean Community) which is made up of 15 Caribbean members.

Advantages of trading blocs

- More free trade means that members should enjoy more consumer choice, higher levels of employment and faster economic growth.
- Firms can exploit economies of scale, since their markets are larger and extra competition will improve product quality and encourage innovation.
- Foreign direct investment (FDI) should increase because foreign firms are keen to locate their operations within a trading bloc to have access to a larger and barrier-free market.

- Closer cooperation should be possible between members. For example countries may share resources, help each other and introduce common standards, laws and customs.

- There will be less cross-border conflict, more peace and more social interaction.

Disadvantages of trading blocs

Members

- They tend to encourage regional free trade rather than global free trade.

- Belonging to a trade bloc can be expensive for the taxpayer. For example the annual cost to the United Kingdom of belonging to the EU is about £66bn.

- Some firms within a trading bloc merge and become too powerful, resulting in regional monopolies and consumer exploitation.

- Countries may start to rely too heavily on trade within the bloc making them vulnerable to changes in prices and demand patterns within the bloc.

- Members may standardise trading practices, laws and other customs which may threaten a nation's culture.

Non-members

- Non-members face trade barriers when selling goods inside the bloc.

- However, in the long run non-members may find new markets. For example when the United Kingdom joined the EU, many of the United Kingdom's Commonwealth trading partners found new markets.

Worked Example

1 The East African Community (EAC) is a trading bloc which includes Burundi, Kenya, Rwanda, Tanzania and Uganda. The population of the bloc is over 124m.

    (a) What is meant by a trading bloc? **(1)**

    (b) Identify **two** advantages to consumers when their country joins a trading bloc. **(2)**

© Edexcel Question paper, May 2012

> **1** *(a)* Trading blocs are groups of countries situated in the same region that join together and make a free trade area. Trade between members will be completely free of all trade barriers.
>
>   *(b)* There will be more consumer choice and lower prices.

TOP TIP

You need to remember the names of specific trading blocs, so it might be helpful to know about one to which your country, or a neighbouring country, belongs.

Revision Questions

1 State **two** reasons why world trade has increased in recent decades. **(2)**

2 Explain **two** disadvantages of trading blocs to their members. **(4)**

3 Do the advantages of a trade bloc outweigh the disadvantages for firms within the bloc? **(6)**

Question 3 © Edexcel Question paper, May 2012

Chapter 48: **The World Trade Organization**

The World Trade Organization

- The World Trade Organization was established in 1995. It replaced a multilateral agreement called the GATT (General Agreement on Tariffs and Trade).

- The WTO aims to promote free trade by persuading countries to abolish trade barriers. It has become closely associated with globalisation.

In 2012, the WTO had 157 members, employed over 600 people and had a budget of over US$200 million.

Activities of the WTO

Figure 48.1 *The main activities of the WTO.*

In November 2009, 15 years after the WTO was established, the WTO reached the milestone of having the 400th trade dispute brought to its dispute-settlement mechanism.

Criticisms of the WTO

The WTO faces criticism from anti-globalisation bodies and environmental groups.

- **It is undemocratic** because the WTO rules are written by and for corporations with inside access to the negotiations. The views of consumers, environmental, human rights and labour organisations are often ignored.

- **It favours the 'rights' of corporations over those of workers.** For example the WTO has said it is illegal for a government to ban a product based on the way it is produced, such as with child labour.

- **It is destroying the environment.** For example the very first WTO panel ruled that a provision of the US Clean Air Act that required both domestic and foreign producers to produce cleaner gasoline was illegal.

- **It favours wealthy nations.** For example negotiators from poor countries are not even invited to meetings and many poor countries do not have enough qualified staff to take part in all of the negotiations.

- **It is causing hardship for poorer nations.** It is argued that the corporate control of food distribution means 800 million people worldwide suffer from malnutrition.

Worked Example

Briefly describe **two** functions of the World Trade Organization. **(4)**

© Edexcel Question paper, May 2012

> One of the main functions of the World Trade Organization (WTO) is to reduce or eliminate barriers to trade. They might do this by organising negotiations between countries that will be involved in the lifting of trade barriers. Another important function is to settle trade disputes between countries. Sometime countries disagree about certain international trading transactions. The WTO will listen to both sides of the argument and help the countries to reach a settlement.

TOP TIP

You need to be able to recall examples of WTO action and its effects. If you want to find some information about current trade disputes, go to the WTO website where any current disputes are listed.

Revision Questions

Sometimes a trade war might develop between nations. This is where one country threatens to impose trade barriers against another. This is done in the belief that the country has been involved in 'sharp' trading practices. However, the nation strikes back by imposing their own barriers.

In 2012, China complained to the WTO about the United States just hours before the United States complained about China. The Chinese government challenged US anti-dumping measures against a wide range of Chinese goods including kitchen appliances, magnets and paper. The US complaint accused Beijing of improperly subsidising exports of vehicles and parts worth US$1bn (£615m) from 2009 to 2011. Some feared that these disputes may lead to a trade war.

1. Explain why a trade war might be a drawback for the two nations involved. **(4)**

2. How might the WTO prevent a trade war? **(2)**

3. Outline **two** possible criticisms of the WTO. **(4)**

Chapter 49: Developed and developing countries

Characteristics of developing countries

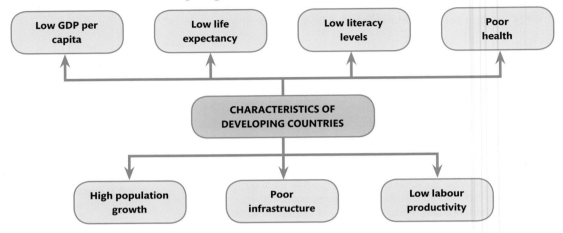

Figure 49.1 *The main characteristics of a developing country.*

There are more than 200 developing countries in the world. Although most of them are in the southern hemisphere they are not all the same.

Trade in developing countries

Examples of recent trends in international trade in developing countries include:

- *An increase in net migration* An increasing number of people are leaving developing countries to find work in the developed countries.

- *Increased FDI in Africa* Many African nations have benefited from an increasing amount of FDI from China.

- *Less reliance on commodities* Globally, the amount of trade in primary goods is falling as a proportion of total trade.

- *Growth in many Eastern European countries* Since the break up of the Soviet Union many Eastern bloc countries have opened their economies and begun to develop.

- *FDI continues to be important* The primary sector—particularly the oil and gas industry—continued to attract FDI to Africa and other countries.

- *Debt cancellation* Developing countries will benefit from the cancellation of the US$40 billion debt which they owed to the World Bank and other organisations.

- *Reduction in barriers* The gains from removing trade barriers are considerable. This has helped developing countries to improve their current account balances significantly.

Trade in developed countries

- **Loss of trade in manufacturing** Manufacturing activities have drifted from Western developed countries to countries such as China and South Korea.

- **More air travel** People continue to travel the world in growing numbers. The emergence of budget airlines has helped.

- **Widening of the development gap** The gap between the rich and poor nations is still widening. For example it is expected that nearly 40 per cent of Africans will still have to live on less than US$1 a day in 2015.

- **Increase in regional trade agreements** There has been a surge in Regional Trade Agreements (RTAs) since the 1990s. The World Bank estimates that about 40 per cent of global trade is done through these trading blocs.

- **Increase in the size of the EU** The most important trading bloc in the world has grown in size recently. In 2012 it had 27 members.

- **Threat of recession** At the end of 2008 and into 2009 the world went into recession. Some developed countries such as Greece, Spain, Italy and Portugal are suffering from high levels of unemployment.

PART 2 Chapter 49: Developed and developing countries

Worked Example

Explain how the cancellation of debt will help a developing country. **(4)**

When debt is cancelled, interest on the debt does not have to be paid. It also means that the debt itself is removed, as it does not have to be repaid. Therefore, the governments of developing countries will have more money to spend on things such as education and the infrastructure. Such spending will create employment and help developing nations to grow. For example a better-educated population means that people will be more employable. An improved infrastructure means better communications. Both of these will help to attract FDI.

TOP TIP
To find more information about trade in both developed and developing nations, go to http://www.tradingeconomics.com.

Revision Questions

1 State **three** possible characteristics of a developing country? **(3)**

2 What is meant by the development gap? **(2)**

3 Explain **two** effects that low labour productivity would have on a developing country. **(4)**

PART 3 Exchange rates

Chapter 50: Exchange rates and their determination

What is an exchange rate?

- The exchange rate is the price of one currency in terms of another.

- When conducting international transactions, payments usually have to be made in another currency. Two examples are shown below:

> **Example 1** How much will it cost a UK business to buy NZ$500,000 of lamb from New Zealand if the exchange rate is £1 = NZ$2.00? The cost in £s will be:
>
> NZ$500,000 ÷ NZ$2.00 = **£250,000**
>
> **Example 2** How many Rupees will be needed for an Italian firm to buy €60,000 of goods from an Indian firm if €1 = Rs70? The cost in Rupees would be:
>
> €60,000 × Rs70 = **Rs4,200,000**

How are exchange rates determined?

- The price of a currency is determined by market forces—supply and demand.

- Currencies are bought and sold like commodities on foreign exchange markets. Banks trade in these markets to obtain currencies for their customers.

- Figure 50.1 shows the supply and demand for British pounds sterling (£). The price of pounds is given in terms of the euro (€). The equilibrium exchange rate is where the supply and demand for pounds are equal. At this point, the price of £1 in euros is €1.25, therefore the exchange rate is £1 = €1.25.

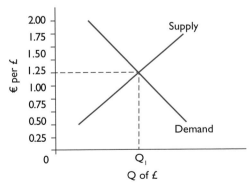

Figure 50.1 *The equilibrium exchange rate.*

Factors affecting the demand for a currency (for example the British £)

- ***The demand for exports*** Firms wishing to buy goods from the United Kingdom must pay in pounds. Therefore the demand for domestic currency is linked to export demand.

- ***Inward foreign direct investment (FDI)*** If a foreign firm wants to build a factory in the United Kingdom, it will need pounds to pay for the materials, labour and other resources required for the construction.

- **Interest** Foreign savers wishing to make a deposit in a UK bank must change their money into pounds. Higher interest rates will attract more savers and thus increase the demand for pounds.

- **Speculation** Speculators buy a particular currency and hope to sell it for a higher price later. If the pound is in favour with speculators, demand for it will increase.

Factors affecting the supply of a currency (for example the British £)

- **The demand for imports** If UK firms buy more imports they will have to buy foreign currency with pounds to pay for them. This increases the supply of pounds.

- **Outward foreign direct investment (FDI)** If British firms invest abroad, the supply of pounds will increase because they must buy foreign currency.

- **Interest rates in other countries** If interest rates are higher in other countries, savers in the United Kingdom may decide to place their money in foreign banks. To do this, they must buy foreign currency with pounds which will increase supply.

- **Speculation** Speculators can also affect the supply of currency. This happens when they decide to sell a particular currency.

Worked Example

1 Figure 50.2 shows the exchange rate of the euro (€) in terms of Kenyan Shillings (KSH).

(a) In which month was the €/KSH exchange rate at its highest? **(1)**

(b) Using Figure 50.2, what was the highest value of 1 euro in terms of Kenyan Shillings in the month identified in (a)? **(1)**

(c) In which month could 10 euros be exchanged for 102.0 Kenyan Shillings? **(1)**

© Edexcel Question paper, June 2011

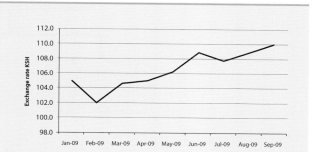

Figure 50.2 Exchange rate: 1 euro (€) to Kenyan Shillings (KSH)

(a) September 2009

(b) KSH110

(c) February 2009

TOP TIP

To help understand exchange rate determination, practise drawing supply and demand diagrams showing the effect on the exchange rate when different factors change.

Revision Questions

1 What is meant by an exchange rate? **(2)**

2 Calculate how much it would cost a French importer, in euros, for US$5m of goods if US$1 = €0.8. **(2)**

3 Explain briefly how an increase in domestic interest rates would increase the exchange rate. **(2)**

4 Draw a supply and demand diagram to show for a country the effect on its exchange rate of an increase in its imports. **(4)**

Chapter 51: **Changing exchange rates and government policy**

Why do exchange rates change?

- Exchange rates change because, like prices, they are determined by market forces and at any time supply and demand conditions can change.

- For example if interest rates in the United Kingdom rise, there will be an increase in demand for pounds as foreigners will be encouraged to make deposits in UK banks.

When the exchange rate falls it is said that there has been a **depreciation** in the exchange rate. When it rises, it can be said that the exchange rate has **appreciated**.

The impact of a falling exchange rate on imports and exports

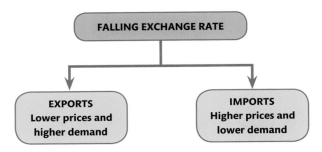

Figure 51.1 *The impact of a falling exchange rate on imports and exports.*

The impact of a rising exchange rate on imports and exports

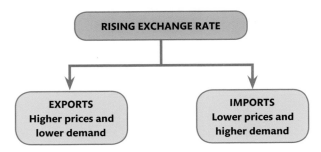

Figure 51.2 *The impact of a rising exchange rate on imports and exports.*

Exchange rates and government policy

How can the government reduce a deficit on the current account?

- One approach is **devaluation**, which is allowing the exchange rate to depreciate.

- If the exchange rate falls, the price of exports falls and the price of imports rises. Therefore, a deficit on the current account should be reduced, because the demand for exports would rise and the demand for imports would fall.

- The government can influence the exchange rate by changing interest rates in the economy. This is explained in Chapter 50.

- There are problems with this policy. The government might not have complete control over the interest rate. In such cases, reducing interest rates may cause inflation.

Exchange rate policy and price elasticity

- The effectiveness of a government's exchange rate policy depends on the price elasticity of demand for imports and exports.

- A current account deficit will only be reduced if the demand for imports and exports are both elastic. Demand must be responsive to price changes.

- A country importing mainly primary goods, such as food, may struggle to reduce imports because demand may be price inelastic.

- A country wanting to boost exports will be more successful if demand for those exports is price elastic.

Worked Example

To what extent will a depreciation in the exchange rate reduce a country's current account deficit? Justify your answer. **(6)**

A government might allow the exchange rate to depreciate by lowering interest rates in the economy. A lower exchange rate will increase the price of imports and reduce the price of exports. This should result in less demand for imports and a greater demand for exports. With falling imports and rising exports, a current account deficit would eventually be reduced. However, the effectiveness of this policy would depend on the price elasticity of demand for imports and exports. For the policy to work, demand for both imports and exports must be price elastic. If a country imports mainly primary goods, such as essential foodstuffs, it may be difficult to reduce imports because demand is likely to be price inelastic. Therefore, it may not be possible to reduce the current account deficit.

TOP TIP ✓

Do not confuse exchange rates with interest rates. They are **very** different. You also need to learn the effects of changes in the exchange rate on the demand for exports and imports. Figure 51.1 and Figure 51.2 will help you.

Revision Questions

1 An appreciation in the exchange rate is likely to
   A raise the price of imports
   B help to reduce unemployment
   C lower the demand for exports
   D lower the prices of exports. *(1)*

2 An importing business will benefit from an appreciation in the exchange rate.
   Explain why this statement is true. *(4)*

3 (a) Calculate how much goods worth AU$600,000 would cost a Spanish importer, in euros, if €1 = AU$1.25. *(2)*

   (b) Calculate the effect on the transaction if a year later the exchange rate is €1 = AU$1.10. *(2)*

   (c) How might Australian businesses be affected by the exchange rate change? *(2)*

Introduction

Examiners are not trying to trick you! The Edexcel International GCSE Economics examination will be fair and will be marked by examiners who want to give you marks for your answer. Students always receive the benefit of any doubt!

The Edexcel International GCSE examination paper

Introduction

- The assessment of this qualification is through a single examination paper lasting two hours and 30 minutes.

- The questions are a mixture of structured, data response, short-answer, multiple-choice and open-ended questions.

- There will be four compulsory questions. Each question will be based on a particular theme which will relate to one of the four sections of the content of the subject. However, due to the nature of economics there may be some overlap between the questions.

- The total number of marks available is 120 (30 for each question).

- You will have no choice of questions in this examination. However, this can be thought of as an advantage. It means that you avoid wasting time in deciding which questions to answer. It will also stop you from starting one question, realising it was the wrong one, and then starting another one. You begin with the first question and work through the whole paper.

Assessment objectives (AO)

To be successful in this examination you need to:

AO1: demonstrate knowledge and understanding of the specified subject content **30–35 per cent**

AO2: apply knowledge and understanding using appropriate terms, concepts, theories and methods to deal with problems and issues **30–35 per cent**

AO3: select, organise, analyse and interpret information from various sources to analyse problems and issues **15–20 per cent**

AO4: evaluate evidence, make reasoned judgements and present conclusions accurately and appropriately **15–20 per cent**

Types of question

- **Short answer questions for 1 mark**. One mark will be awarded for answering multiple-choice questions, labelling diagrams, reading diagrams, giving examples and filling in missing words.

- **Short answer questions for 2 marks**. Two marks will be awarded for identifying two examples, writing definitions and giving brief explanations.

- **Questions for 3 or 4 marks**. Three or four marks will be awarded for answers that require more detailed explanations, perhaps with examples, and drawing diagrams. Such questions may require application and analysis.

- **Long-answer questions for 5 or 6 marks**. Five or six marks will be awarded for answering questions that require both analysis and evaluation. Such questions will usually require you to give an opinion, or make a judgement, and to support your answer with reasons.

Note: The above descriptions are general guidelines. There may be variations in the actual examination. Examples of all of these question styles are used in this Revision Guide.

The language of exams

Examination questions may contain a variety of different **command** words. These are the words that tell you what is expected of you when answering the question. In economics, they suggest to you which skills are being tested. Some examples, their meaning and an example of how they might be used in the Edexcel International GCSE Economics examination are given below.

Knowledge and understanding

Certain command words are used to find out what you know about the subject. They are testing your knowledge and understanding.

- **Define** – to state the exact meaning of a term or a phrase
  Define income elasticity of demand.

- **What is meant by** – to clarify something
  What is meant by a trading bloc?

- **How** – to present an account of something
  How much tax was owed to the United Kingdom in 2009?

- **Briefly describe** – to give an account or portrayal of something
  Briefly describe two functions of the World Trade Organization.

- **Identify** – to give a particular example of something
  Identify two main items of government expenditure.

- **Give** – means to write something down. Sometimes followed by 'an example' or 'an account of'.
  Give an example of an occupation in each of the following sectors:
  (i)   *Primary*
  (ii) *Secondary*
  (iii) *Tertiary*

Application and analysis

Some command words are used to encourage you to apply knowledge to a given situation, to work out why something has happened, and to give reasons for something that has happened. Such words are designed to encourage you to demonstrate application and analytical skills.

- **Explain or briefly explain** – to make a concept, idea or viewpoint clear. It may involve giving an illustration of the meaning or providing examples. It is often followed by the word 'how' or 'why'
  Briefly explain two reasons why an increase in the rate of interest might lead to an increase in the level of unemployment.

- **Calculate** – to work out mathematically, for example usually numerically, but sometimes from a graph
  Calculate Julia's total costs for April. Show your workings.

- **Examine** – to investigate closely to find out the 'truth' of the situation as if you were carrying out an investigation
  Examine how a change in a government's spending could increase growth in a country.

Analysis and evaluation

Certain command words are used to encourage you to make a judgement or to evaluate a particular statement.

- **Assess** – an invitation to measure or place a value on the importance of something
  Assess the effects of an ageing population on the firms in an economy.

- **Do you think** – to comment on or give an opinion on the basis of evidence
  Do mergers between firms producing similar goods and services always benefit consumers? Give reasons for your answer.

- **To what extent (does/do)** – to make a judgement or to measure
  To what extent is international borrowing by a developing country likely to lead to an increase in their standard of living? Give reasons for your answer.

- **Do you agree with this statement** – this is very similar to 'Do you think'. A judgement with justification is required here.
  An increase in the minimum wage rate will benefit only a small number of people in the country. Do you agree with this statement? Give reasons for your answer.

- **Discuss** – to consider a controversial statement or to review an area which might have two or more points of view
  Discuss whether the costs of privatisation outweigh its benefits to the economy.

Things to do and not to do in examinations

To do

- Read the question carefully two or three times.

- Look at the command words carefully. For example evaluation is not necessary if the command word is 'define'.

- Answer the question set by the examiner, not the one that you wish they had asked!

- Always attempt **ALL** questions. Examiners cannot award marks if the space is blank—your knowledge will be greater than you realise!

- Divide your time equally between each of the four questions. This is because every question carries the same number of marks.

- Present your answers neatly. This will make it easier for the examiner to award marks for your answer.

- Show formulae and all working out for the questions that require calculation.

- When evaluating, it may be possible to draw a number of different conclusions. However, examiners may be less concerned with the particular conclusion that you have reached. Very often in economics there is no exclusively 'right' or 'wrong' answer. There are often several different ways of achieving the same objective. Therefore, examiners are more interested in whether you have actually made a judgement, and also in the quality of your argument which supports your judgement.

Not to do

Do not:

- stay up late revising for an exam. A good night's sleep will help you to perform better in an exam.

- arrive late for the exam—this will put you under pressure.

- forget your equipment.

- panic if your mind appears to go blank. Once you start answering questions your memory will start to work again—look at key words in the question; this will help.

- spend too long on questions which carry a few marks. Unless you have unusually large handwriting, the space provided on the paper will be plenty.

- use shorthand in your answers—the examiner may not understand this and marks may be lost.

- become bogged down with a question—move quickly on to the next one if you can't think of anything else to write. You can always go back to add something later.

Dealing with exam stress

Your International GCSE exams are important to you. This is why you might experience stress. This is quite usual. However, too much stress can be bad for you.

During your revision and examination period you may become stressed for the following reasons:

- loneliness
- fear of failure
- overwork
- pressure from parents or other people
- guilt
- boredom.

People suffering from stress may show it in the some of the following ways. They may:

- want to be alone
- have difficulty in sleeping
- lose the ability to concentrate
- become very emotional or sensitive
- lose self-esteem and feel depressed
- become irritable and short-tempered
- suffer from headaches, skin problems and so on.

The diagram below has some tips for managing stress during the revision and examination period.

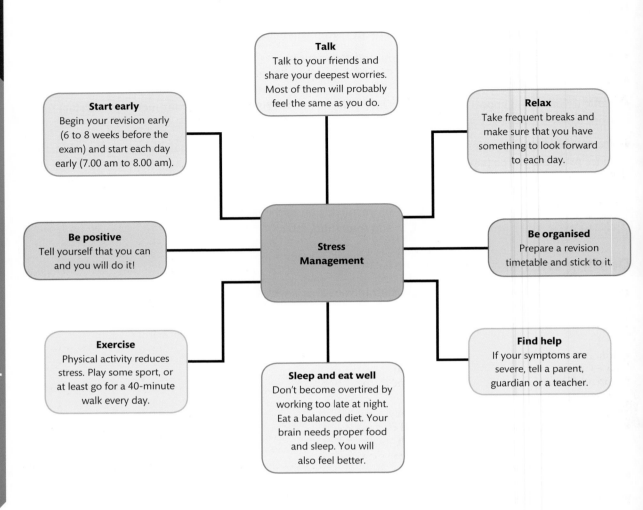

Talk
Talk to your friends and share your deepest worries. Most of them will probably feel the same as you do.

Start early
Begin your revision early (6 to 8 weeks before the exam) and start each day early (7.00 am to 8.00 am).

Relax
Take frequent breaks and make sure that you have something to look forward to each day.

Be positive
Tell yourself that you can and you will do it!

Stress Management

Be organised
Prepare a revision timetable and stick to it.

Exercise
Physical activity reduces stress. Play some sport, or at least go for a 40-minute walk every day.

Sleep and eat well
Don't become overtired by working too late at night. Eat a balanced diet. Your brain needs proper food and sleep. You will also feel better.

Find help
If your symptoms are severe, tell a parent, guardian or a teacher.

Good luck!

Aggregate demand   total demand in an economy: consumption, investment, government expenditure, and exports minus imports

Anti-competitive or restrictive trade practices   attempts by firms to restrict or prevent competition

Average costs   the cost per unit of output; it is equal to total cost divided by the number of units of output

Balance of payments   record of all of the transactions resulting from international trade

Barriers to entry   obstacles that might discourage a firm from entering a market

Capital intensive   where production relies more heavily on machinery relative to labour

Cartel   a group of firms or countries join together to agree on pricing or output levels in an industry; **collusion** is where informal agreements between firms restrict competition

Complementary goods   goods purchased together because they are consumed together

Consumer price index   used in the United Kingdom and the Eurozone, it is a measure of the general price level excluding housing costs

Demand deficient (cyclical) unemployment   unemployment caused by falling demand in the economic cycle

Demand   the amount of a good bought at given prices over a period of time; a **Demand curve** is a line on a graph which shows how much of a good will be bought at different prices; **Derived demand** is the demand that arises because there is demand for another good

Depression or slump   the bottom of an economic cycle, when GDP falls with significant increases in unemployment; **Recession** a less severe form of depression

Diseconomies of scale   rising average costs when output rises

Division of labour   the breaking down of the production process into small parts with each worker allocated a part of the process

Dumping   where an overseas firm sells large quantities of a product below cost in the domestic market

Economic policy instruments   economic variables such as interest rates, taxation rates and government expenditure that governments can adjust in managing the economy

Economies of scale   falling average costs due to expansion

Effective demand   the amount of a good people can afford to buy, and would buy, at any given price over a period of time

Efficiency   minimising costs and the use of resources

Entrepreneur   an individual who organises the other factors of production and risks their own money in a business venture

Equilibrium price   the price where supply and demand are equal

Excess demand   where demand is greater than supply and there are shortages in the market

Excess supply   where supply is greater than demand and there are unsold goods in the market

Exchange rate   the price of one currency in terms of the currency of another country; a **devaluation** is the fall in the value of a currency; an **appreciation** is when the exchange rate rises

Exports   are goods and services sold overseas; **imports** are goods and services bought from overseas

Externalities   the spillover effects of consumption or production; they affect others and may be positive or negative

Factors of production   the resources used to produce goods and services. They include land, labour, capital and enterprise

Fixed capital   the stock of 'man-made' resources such as machines and tools used to help make goods and services

Fixed costs   costs that do not vary with the level of output

Foreign direct investment   business investment undertaken by a firm in another country, such as building a factory

Frictional unemployment   workers are unemployed briefly while they move from one job to another

Gross Domestic Product (GDP)   is an internationally recognised measure of a country's national income

Human capital   the value of the workforce or of an individual worker

Income elasticity of demand   the responsiveness of demand to a change in income

Inferior good   a good for which demand will fall if income rises or will increase if income falls

Inflation   is a general and persistent rise in prices; **deflation** is period when the level of aggregate demand is falling

Inverse relationship between price and quantity demanded   when price rises quantity demanded falls; when price falls the quantity demanded rises

Labour intensive   where production relies more heavily on labour relative to machinery

Labour   the people used in the production of goods and services

Macroeconomics the study of the whole economy; **microeconomics** is the study of individual parts of an economy

Market failure where markets lead to inefficiency

Market system or price mechanism the automatic determination of prices and the allocation of resources through markets operating in the economy

Market-clearing price the price in a market where the amount supplied exactly equals the amount demanded

Minimum wage a minimum amount per hour which most workers are entitled to be paid

Mixed economy an economy where goods and services are provided by both the public and private sectors

Monetarists economists who believe that there is a strong link between growth in the money supply and inflation

Monetary policy the use of interest rates and the money supply to control aggregate demand in the economy

Monopoly a situation where there is one seller in a market; a **natural monopoly** is where it is less costly in an industry for one firm, rather than many, to produce a good or service and supply the whole market

Multinationals are companies that have significant production or service operations in at least two countries

National income the value of income, output or expenditure over a period of time

Normal good a good for which demand will rise if income rises or fall if income falls

Oligopoly is a market dominated by a few large firms

Opportunity cost when choosing between different alternatives it is the benefit lost from the next best alternative

Price elastic demand a change in the price results in a more than proportionate change in demand

Price elasticity of demand the responsiveness of demand to a change in price

Price elasticity of supply the responsiveness of supply to a change in price

Price inelastic demand a change in the price results in a proportionately smaller change in demand

Primary industry production involving extraction of materials from the earth including mining, forestry, fishing and agriculture

Private sector the provision of goods and services by businesses that are owned by individuals or groups of individuals

Privatisation the transfer of public sector resources to the private sector

Product differentiation an attempt by a firm to make its product distinct from that of its competitor

Production a process which involves converting resources into goods and services; a **Production possibility curve** (PPC) is a line which shows the different combinations of two goods an economy can produce when all available resources are used

Productivity the amount of output per unit of input

Profit maximisation making the largest amount of profit possible in a period of time

Public goods goods that are not likely to be provided by the private sector

Public sector government organisations that provide goods and services in the economy

Secondary industry production involving the conversion of raw materials into finished and semi-finished goods

Social benefits and costs the benefits and costs of an economic activity to society as well as to the individual or firm

Specialisation the production of a limited range of goods by individuals, firms, regions or countries

Structural unemployment caused by changes in the structure of an economy such as a decline in an industry

Subsidy a grant given to producers, usually to encourage the production of a certain good

Substitute goods goods bought as an alternative to another good that performs the same function

Supply is the amount sellers are prepared to sell at given prices over a period of time; a **Supply curve** is a line on a graph that shows how much of a good sellers are willing to supply at different prices

Tariffs or customs duties a tax on imports to make them more expensive to sell

Tertiary industry production of services in the economy

Total costs fixed cost and variable cost added together

Total revenue the amount of money generated from the sale of goods that is calculated by multiplying price by quantity

Trading bloc a group of countries situated in the same region that join together and enjoy trade free from tariffs, quotas and other trade barriers

Variable costs costs that rise or fall as output levels are increased or decreased, respectively

Voluntary unemployment resulting from people choosing not to work

Headings in **bold** are glossary terms.

Index